GOD
FOR THE
REST OF US

EXPERIENCE UNBELIEVABLE LOVE, UNLIMITED HOPE, AND UNCOMMON GRACE

VINCE ANTONUCCI

Tyndale House Publishers, Inc.
Carol Stream, Illinois

Visit Tyndale online at www.tyndale.com.

Visit Vince Antonucci at www.vinceantonucci.com and www.godfortherestofus.com.

TYNDALE and Tyndale's quill logo are registered trademarks of Tyndale House Publishers, Inc.

God for the Rest of Us: Experience Unbelievable Love, Unlimited Hope, and Uncommon Grace

Designed by Ron Kaufmann

Edited by Jane Vogel

Published in association with the literary agency of the Gates Group, 1403 Walnut Lane, Louisville, Kentucky, 40223.

Library of Congress Cataloging-in-Publication Data

Antonucci, Vince.
   God for the rest of us : experience unbelievable love, unlimited hope, and uncommon grace / Vince Antonucci.
     pages cm
   Includes bibliographical references.
   ISBN 978-1-4964-0716-0 (sc)
  1. God (Christianity)—Love. 2. God (Christianity)—Love—Biblical teaching. I. Title.
  BT140.A58 2015
  231'.6—dc23   2015012960

Printed in the United States of America

21	20	19	18	17	16	15
7	6	5	4	3	2	1

In this theology, we can never give up on anyone because our God
was one who had a particularly soft spot for sinners.

BISHOP DESMOND TUTU

CONTENTS

FOREWORD

ONE OF MY NEPHEWS was telling me about his recent experience at a car dealership. He was planning on taking advantage of a year-end special. He had a buddy drop him off at the dealership, confident he would be driving home in his new truck. He took a test drive and worked with a salesperson to find the right color with the right options. He was then asked to fill out a loan application. As he began answering the different questions, he started to get a little nervous. The dealership checked his credit, and since he didn't have any, he didn't qualify for the loan. He called his mom and asked her to come pick him up.

As my nephew gets older he'll learn to be skeptical of such offers. The year-end special was a great deal, but only for certain people. You have to meet the right criteria. You have to have a certain amount of resources. It was a great deal for *some* people, but not for *all* people.

A few years ago I went to the home of an older couple who were interested in becoming a part of the church where I pastor. Neither of them had grown up in church, and they had only attended services where I preach a few times. They had a few questions about the church, and then with complete sincerity and spirit of humility, the wife asked, "Is there an application I need to fill out be a member of your church?" Before I had a chance to respond, her husband jumped in and asked a question with a little more cynicism: "What I want to know is, how much does it cost?" They assumed there was an application process and a price tag for being a part the church.

I quickly explained to them that they didn't have to pass a test, and that being a Christian and a part of the church was free. I talked to them about the love of God and his gift of grace through Jesus Christ. But they were both skeptical. It seemed too good to be true, and they were convinced that there was some fine print they weren't being told about.

As a pastor, I regularly talk to people who don't think their application for God's love and grace will be approved. It may be a great deal for some people, but not for them. They know their own histories. They have ideas about their value and worth, and they feel certain that they won't qualify. I suppose, if I'm being honest, these aren't just stories that people share with me; there have been times when that's been my story as well. I know my own sins and failures. I know the debt I have accumulated, and there are some days when I have a hard time believing God loves me.

I love this book because it convinces me that God's love is greater and deeper than I dared imagine. It challenges me to share that extravagant love with others. There is no shortage of books out there that share ideas and commentary about

God's love. This book doesn't just tell me about God's love; it shows me what God's love looks like when it's lived out in real life.

I have known Vince Antonucci for well over a decade, and I love getting to spend time with him, because he always has the most incredible stories of how God's love is impacting the people he pastors in Las Vegas. In these pages, you will read real-life stories from the people Vince and his church minister to—stories that will have you laughing and crying, that will lead you to realize no one is beyond God's grace, that will make you fall in love with God for the first time, or all over again.

Kyle Idleman
author of *Not a Fan* and *The End of Me*

1

GOD FOR THE REST OF US

PUTTING DUCT TAPE over our mouths was a nice touch. But it did get us accused of child abuse. Ah, the perils of shock art for Jesus.

We were on Fremont Street. Fremont is the "old Strip" in Las Vegas and still the most visited attraction in Sin City. It's where the bullhorn Christians hang out and yell. They stand on soapboxes, informing people that their final destination will be hotter than a 115-degree August day in the desert outside Vegas.

One full-time hatemonger on Fremont is a guy who stands proudly holding up a huge sign with the title "WWJD?" Just below the letters it says, "Who Will Jesus Destroy?"

Underneath is a list of all kinds of sinners. Some are a bit more scandalous—abortionists, murderers, oppressive communist despots. But take heart, you're on the list too. It includes liars, gossips, cheats, the lust filled. The man yells and angles his sign at everyone who passes—drunk guys from Wisconsin, the handicapped homeless lady shuffling by, businessmen from Poughkeepsie, the elderly ladies from the church in Iowa who are in town for the knitting convention.

At some point it's not enough just to shake your head in sadness at the guy holding the sign. At some point you have to make a sign of your own, and we decided to do it. That's not entirely true. We actually decided to go with flyers because it seemed like a more personal touch—and we could also be sure to avoid splinters.

Our flyer's title? "WDJL?" Just below the letters it says, "Who Does Jesus Love?" Underneath is a list of, well . . . it's the exact same list as on the "Who Will Jesus Destroy?" sign. We realized that copying the list would lose us creativity points, but we wanted to make sure everyone made the connection to the bullhorn, hatemonger guy.

To add creativity, we put duct tape over our mouths as we handed out the flyers right in front of the bullhorn, hatemonger guy. Under the list of people Jesus loves, our flyers proclaimed:

It's very common to find "street preachers" here on Fremont Street, loudly declaring who *God hates*. There's a problem with that, and it's that **GOD**

LOVES. The Bible says that "God IS love" and that he sent Jesus not to condemn, but because of and in love.

The truth is that *God loves* . . . homosexuals, gamblers, strippers, abortionists, prostitutes, addicts, and you.

And so we apologize for anything you've ever heard that would lead you to believe otherwise. The reason they spread a message of hate is because there is power in hate. But we have chosen the way of Jesus, the way of love, and find it far more powerful.

We have taped our mouths shut as a symbolic way of offsetting the verbal abuse you may have heard in the past and may hear tonight.

So, in this battle of the signs (okay, it was a battle of a sign versus flyers, but at least we didn't get splinters—but don't ask me about all the paper cuts), who was right? Was God smiling down on bullhorn, hatemonger guy or on the duct-taped crusaders of love? For the answer, we need to go to Jesus.

Stories

Jesus loved to tell stories.

His stories made people angry. People hated him for his stories.

You could argue that it was his stories that got him killed.

One time Jesus was surrounded by two very different

groups of people. One group was made up of "tax collectors and sinners."

The tax collectors were Jews who had betrayed God and his people by siding with the Romans. The Romans were trying to take over the world, and their strategy was violence. They would come into a Jewish town and demand that everyone worship Caesar. Those who refused because they were faithful to God would be executed. The invaders would then tax those left alive and use the money to fund their massive army, invade more towns, and kill more innocent Jewish people. The Romans hired Jews to collect the taxes from their own people—Jewish money funding the murder of more Jews.

The sinners were, well, sinners. We know that we're all sinners, but you've got to be on the other side of awful for it to be written on your name tag at social functions. These weren't garden-variety sinners. These were "notoriously evil people as well as those who refused to follow the Mosaic Law as interpreted by the teachers of the law. The term was commonly used of tax collectors, adulterers, robbers and the like."[1]

Why were the tax collectors and sinners gathered around Jesus? We're told, "to hear [him]."[2] They loved Jesus and his stories.

Think about that for a minute. When God came to earth, the people who wanted to be around him were tax collectors, adulterers, and robbers. It was the sinners who loved to be around Jesus.

A second group was stalking the periphery of this notorious band of sinners—"the Pharisees and the teachers of the law."[3] They weren't gathered around Jesus because they loved to be around him. They were gathered around Jesus because they hated it that the *sinners* loved to be around him. They were the ones who hated Jesus' stories, who thought murder was the best way to stop him from telling his scandalous little parables. We're told that they were muttering to one another. Personally, I don't think I've ever been around a group of mutterers, but it doesn't sound like a fun time. What they were muttering was, "This man welcomes sinners and eats with them."[4] They found Jesus' actions offensive.

In response, Jesus told a story. Actually, he told three stories.

The First Two Stories

The first two stories are about people who lose things—a shepherd who loses a sheep and a woman who loses a coin. Both have plenty more. In fact, it's a bit of a surprise that they even notice that one is missing.

My parents had two kids. Once when I was about six years old and my sister, Lisa, was four, our parents took us out for dinner.* Afterward they put us in the backseat of the car. They did not buckle us in. This was the mid-seventies, and my parents now tell me that no one put seat belts on

---

*I believe it was Arthur Treacher's Fish & Chips. (Have you ever heard of Arthur Treacher's? Have you ever been to Arthur Treacher's? If so, let me know. There's a support group I can tell you about.)

their kids back then. I believe they just didn't care about us. My parents got in the front, started the car, and popped in the 8-track tape.* Knowing my parents, it was probably *Neil Diamond's Greatest Hits.*** So the music filled the car ("Hands, touching hands, reachin' out, touchin' me, touchin' you. Sweet Caroline . . ."***). My father shifted into drive and pulled out of the parking spot. It turned out they hadn't shut my sister's door very well, so it swung open. My sister was leaning against it and fell out of the car. The door quietly swung shut. My parents didn't notice. And I didn't say a word! I just waved good-bye out the back window. "Good times never seemed so good. I've been inclined to believe they never would." We turned out of the parking lot and started driving down the road. Finally, my father looked back, did a double take, frantically surveyed the backseat of the car, and then yelled, "Where's Lisa?" I pointed back at the parking lot. "But . . . now . . . I . . ." My father slammed on the brakes, whipped the car around, went back, and found my sister sobbing in the parking lot.****

My parents had only two kids, but it took them a while to realize that one of us was missing . . . from the car! But the shepherd and the woman in Jesus' stories immediately recognize that something is missing.

And they not only realize it; they care. In fact, each goes on an all-out search-and-rescue mission. And when they find

---

*If you're younger than 40, call your parents and ask them what an 8-track is.
**If you're younger than 40, call your parents and ask them who Neil Diamond is.
***You just sang, "Bum, bum, bum"! Admit it!
****She always was a crybaby.

what's lost, they party like it's 1999. They're on their cell phones, calling their neighbors, and inviting them into the celebration.

It all seems over the top. Borderline absurd. But then Jesus inserts the knife. "In the same way, I tell you, there is rejoicing in the presence of the angels of God over one sinner who repents."[5] These aren't just cute stories. They are more of Jesus' parabolic grenades, and it's obvious that Jesus was responding to the mutterers. The stories aren't really about a lost sheep and a lost coin. These stories show that the reason Jesus welcomed sinners and ate with them was because those sinners were actually God's lost children.

When our kids were younger, my wife and I took them to a big water park. Our son was five and our daughter was about to turn three, so we spent the day in the kiddie pools. Each pool had slides and all kinds of fun stuff. We played in one pool for a while and then walked about a hundred yards to a second kiddie pool, where we let the kids splash around. We then walked another hundred yards to the next one. My kids were repeatedly going down one big slide. My wife walked over to the other side of the pool where they had a big, mushroom-shaped umbrella shower. My son, Dawson, came down the slide and asked, "Where's Mom?"

"She's over by the mushroom-water-shower-umbrella thingy," I answered.

"Can I go get her?" he asked.

"Sure," I told him, "Go ahead."

About five minutes later I grabbed my daughter and said, "Let's go get Mommy and Dawson."

So we went over to the shower. My wife was still under it, but all by herself.

I asked, "Where's Dawson?"

She was confused. "What are you talking about?"

"I sent him over about five minutes ago."

"I haven't seen him."

I started looking all over the kiddie pool. I didn't see him. I thought, *Don't freak out, Vince, he's here. Um, he's wearing a blue bathing suit.* I looked for a blue bathing suit. No. *Okay. It's okay. Look for light brown hair.* No. *Maybe he's in one of the slides.* No. I finally yelled, "Dawson!"

It had now been about ten minutes since we had seen our son. I continued to look. Soon it was fifteen minutes. I thought, *I am never going to see my son again. I'm never going to hold my son again.* I started totally freaking out.

The kiddie pool was in a sort of valley. I ran up the stairs to the sidewalk so I could have a better view of the whole pool. I looked down. Dawson was not there. My heart started racing. My throat was closing up. My head was pounding. I looked again. He was not there. Blue bathing suit? No. Light brown hair? No. In one of the slides? No. I wanted to *die*.

I looked up the sidewalk to my left. No. I looked down the sidewalk to my right. No. I looked in the pool again. No. It had now been close to twenty minutes. I again looked up the sidewalk to my left. Far down the path I saw what seemed to be a light-brown-haired kid weaving between people. I couldn't see the color of the bathing suit. I called out, "Dawson? Dawson!"

Then I yelled again, "Dawson!"

Finally the light-brown-haired boy looked up, and it was my son. "Dawson!"

He saw me, and his face went white. I ran toward him. He ran toward me. We met. He dove into my arms, crying. I asked, "Where were you?"

"I went to find Mommy," he said. "I thought she was at the pool we were at before."

I said, "You went all the way to the other pool by yourself?" And I held him. And I held him. And I held him. And I realized in that moment that I understood, just a little, what it's like to be God. The way I felt about my son, wondering if I'd ever see or hold him again, is the way God feels about all of his children who have wandered away from him.[7] I think of Jeremiah 4, where God says, "Oh, my anguish, my anguish! I writhe in pain. Oh, the agony of my heart! My heart pounds within me, I cannot keep silent."[6] Pretty intense talk coming from God, and it makes you wonder: What is God so tormented about? He tells us: "My people are fools; they do not know me. They are senseless children; they have no understanding. They are skilled in doing evil; they know not how to do good."[8]

But God doesn't reject his senseless children. His heart is broken, and he offers an invitation: "If you, Israel, will return, then return to me."[9]

That's why Jesus came. It was an all-out search-and-rescue mission. It was to get God's lost children home.

Prodigal: The Trilogy Complete

For the Pharisees and the teachers of the law, the first two stories were bad enough. But Jesus proceeds to tell a third story, and it's worse.

We call this story the parable of the Prodigal Son, but as one of my favorite Bible teachers, Timothy Keller, points out, there are some problems with that.

First, the story features *three* characters, not just a son.

And second, most people don't know what the word *prodigal* means, even if they think they do.

In the movie *The Princess Bride*, Inigo Montoya says to a character named Vizzini about his incessant use of the word *inconceivable*, "You keep using that word. I do not think it means what you think it means."

Sometimes words don't mean what we think they mean.

A lot of people use the word *nauseous*. As in, "I'm feeling nauseous." And they think it means "to feel sick," but it doesn't. Nauseous actually means to *cause* nausea. So if you eat a whole chocolate cake and say, "I feel nauseous," what you're actually saying is that you're causing the people around you to feel sick.*

Or the word *literally*. People misuse it all the time. It means "truly or actually." Sports announcers will say, "In the fourth quarter, LeBron James literally put the team on his back and carried them to victory!" Really? 'Cause that's a basketball game I want to see! Or people say, "I'm literally

---

*Which, I guess, you might be.

starving to death." You keep using that word. I do not think it means what you think it means.*

Sometimes words lose their meanings when they're translated into another language. At one point Pepsi had a slogan, "Come alive! You're in the Pepsi generation," which they learned, too late, was translated into Chinese as "Pepsi brings your ancestors back from the grave." When KFC opened its first franchise in Beijing, the restaurant's famous slogan was translated from "Finger-lickin' good," to "Eat your fingers off." (Yum!) Coors Brewing Company also ran into problems when trying to translate a slogan. After launching their "Turn it loose" campaign in Spain, they discovered that this translates to "Suffer from diarrhea"! (Yum?)

So we say this story is about a *prodigal* son. We call the son in this story a prodigal. You may have used the word. But I do not think it means what you think it means. Somewhere along the way, something was lost in translation.

The word *prodigal* means "wastefully extravagant." That's what the word *literally* means. Wastefully extravagant.

Jesus' third story in this trilogy is one we call the parable of the Prodigal Son. And it seems appropriate for me to write about the idea of a prodigal because in 2009 I moved to become sort of a missionary to Las Vegas. A year later we started a church right in the heart of Sin City. And Las Vegas is the land of prodigals.

---

* Although one of the amazing things about the English language is that if enough people misuse a word, eventually the "wrong" meaning makes it into the dictionary along with the original meaning.

Look around Las Vegas, especially the Strip, and you'll see that the city has been extravagantly wasteful. Why? Because they hope tourists who come will return the favor. Vegas's thinking is: We will be extravagantly wasteful in spending money in order to lure you to Sin City so you will be extravagantly wasteful in *losing* money.

And everywhere you look around the city, you see prodigals. Let me introduce you to some of the prodigals I've met in Las Vegas:

Peter was in his fifties and going nowhere fast. Seeking meaning, he explored Eastern religions. He was still confused spiritually, but the one conclusion he had come to was that reincarnation is real.

Hector grew up in a Las Vegas gang. It was basically all he ever knew.

Dharma was a dancer in several Las Vegas shows, including at least one where she danced topless. Her husband worked in IT for a pornography company.

Randy was an addict who called our church to find out if we had a 12-step program.

David seemed to be a young entrepreneurial businessman who was doing well for himself. The truth is that he was wanted by the police in another state where he had been a drug dealer.

Julie was a pole-dancing instructor.

Scott and Cooper were atheists.

Frank was a strip-club bouncer and leg breaker raising two teenage sons on his own.

Sal was a casino pitboss.

Jack was an alcoholic taxi driver who was considering suicide because his life had bottomed out.

Cici was a crystal meth addict who for years had been a member of the Order, a white supremacist neo-Nazi hate group. She had been married nine times and shot fourteen times.

Sandy was a Britney Spears impersonator determined to never go back to church because she believed it was a negative place filled with judgmental people.

I've become convinced that all these people are looking for love. You might think of being in a gang, dancing topless, or doing (or selling) drugs as a rejection of God's love, but I believe the people who do those things are searching for it. I think you are too. And so am I. That's why I wrote this book. Because we underestimate the scope and the power of God's love. We think there are people's lives to whom it doesn't apply. We might even include ourselves in that list. And we don't grasp how powerful God's love can be when it's applied to a person's life, so some of us may never let it take hold of us. That brings us back to Jesus' third story. To the inner circle of tax collectors and sinners and to the muttering periphery of Pharisees and teachers of the law, Jesus tells the story of the Prodigal Son.

It starts out with a father of two sons. The younger son comes to his father and demands his inheritance. Basically he tells his father that he wishes the father were dead, but lacking that good fortune, he'd at least like to spend the rest of his life pretending it was the case. The father gives him what he asks for, and his younger son goes off and wastes it all. He lives out his every sinful fantasy until he finds himself out of money and physically in the same squalor his soul has been residing in. Staring up from rock bottom, he has a change of heart. He decides to return home. He doesn't imagine his father will take him back as a son, but he hopes his father will give him a job working on the farm. As he makes the journey home, he practices a speech: "Father, I have sinned against heaven and against you. I am no longer worthy to be called your son; make me like one of your hired servants."[10]

What he doesn't know is that since he left, his father has been sitting on the front porch, staring down the road, hoping this day would come. So "while he was still a long way off, his father saw him and was filled with compassion for him; he ran to his son, threw his arms around him and kissed him."[11] The father welcomes his son back into the family and throws a party to celebrate his return.

Consider this for a moment. Think about the absolute worst thing you did growing up. How did your parents respond? I'm guessing they didn't throw you a celebratory party. "Our son got his girlfriend pregnant. Come to a party in his honor!" "Our daughter wrapped our car around a telephone pole on the way home from a party she wasn't allowed to be at. Come celebrate with us!" "We found drugs and pornography in our son's room. We're renting a ballroom and hiring the best band in town. You won't believe the amazing cake we got him!"

Nope.

That's not what they did.

No matter how loving your parents may have been, it doesn't even begin to compare to the astonishing grace of God.

And that's what Jesus is trying to communicate in this story. The father represents God. The son takes half his father's money, leaves home, and spends it all on prostitutes and partying. The son comes home in reproachable dishonor. And the father throws him a party.

It seems like that should be the absurd but happy ending of the story, but Jesus continues, and this is where he really twists the knife.

Suddenly the older brother appears. He's indignant that his father has accepted his wayward brother back into the family. And he cannot believe the audacity of his father actually throwing a party for him. He says, "Look! All these years I've been slaving for you and never disobeyed your orders. Yet you never gave me even a young goat so I could celebrate with my friends. But when this son of yours who has squandered your property with prostitutes comes home, you kill the fattened calf for him!"[12]

Then Jesus ends the story—looking, I imagine, with sadness at the Pharisees and teachers of the law glaring at him from a distance—by sharing the response of the father to his indignant son. "'My son,' the father said, 'you are always with me, and everything I have is yours. But we had to celebrate and be glad, because this brother of yours was dead and is alive again; he was lost and is found.'"[13]

So people call this the parable of the Prodigal Son. And originally the idea was probably that the younger son was "extravagantly wasteful" with his father's money.

But since nowadays we don't attach the original, actual definition to *prodigal*, when we call the younger son the prodigal, what we're probably thinking is that he was the son who rejected his father's love.

And he *did*. When he asked for his father's inheritance, he wasn't just requesting an advance on his money. He was telling his father that he wished his father were dead. He was saying, "Father, I don't want *you*. I just want your stuff."

But let's be clear: the older son *also* rejected his father and his father's love. The younger son rejected his father through a journey of self-discovery. He thought there was pleasure to be found out in the world and that finding it would mean he wouldn't need his father. The older rejected his father through morality. He thought he was so good that he really didn't need his father.[14] And like his brother, the older son didn't really want his father either; he just wanted his father's stuff. When he learned of the party, the older son angrily complained that his father had never given him a young goat so he could have a party with his friends.*

And actually, the older brother and his rejection of the father is more the point of Jesus' story. We feel like the story is more about the younger son. But the reason Jesus told this story was to address the objections of the religious legalists.

---

*'Cause there ain't no party like a young goat party, 'cause a young goat party don't stop.

They couldn't understand why Jesus was teaching that God was for these rebellious sinners. With the character of the older son, Jesus was trying to show them that they also had rejected God. Rather than rejecting him through bad behavior like the "sinners," these legalists had rejected God through good behavior that led them to believe they were beyond the need of God's grace.

But the star prodigal of this story is . . . the *father*. *Prodigal* means extravagantly wasteful, and the father in the story is the most extravagantly wasteful character of all. The younger son wished him dead, but the father gave the money to him anyway. The older son completely disrespected him, but the father told him, "Everything I have is yours." The father in this story is the prodigal father. He is extravagantly wasteful with his love.

The point of Jesus' story is that God is for everyone. Some won't receive his love, so you could argue it's wasted on them. But God offers it nonetheless.

The stories of the prodigals I meet in Las Vegas could be viewed as a testament of God's wasteful love. Honestly, *I* serve as a living illustration. I think of all the love God has squandered on me because I stubbornly refused it and also of how radically his love has transformed my life when I willingly received it. And I wonder about you. Can you look back on years of love God has wasted on you because you were unaware or unwilling to accept it? Maybe you're ready to have your life revolutionized by the most powerful force in the universe—the limitless love of God.

Pouring Love

Literally (as in actually, truly) as I was writing that last paragraph, there was a knock on our front door. Our neighbor was standing there, and he said, "This is not a complaint, just an observation. But there is water from your yard pouring under the wall between us and into my yard. I'm afraid if it continues, the wall is going to come down. Just thought you might want to know."

Um, yeah, I want to know!

Jesus left heaven and came to earth to pour God's love from his place into ours, from his heart into ours, from his life into ours. His goal, in a sense, was for the dividing wall to come down so heaven would fill up the earth.

Jesus came to pour God's love all over the place.

Philip Yancey, in his book *What's So Amazing about Grace?*, tells the unfortunately true story about a time a woman went to see a counselor in Chicago and confessed that she was a drug addict who prostituted herself to get money to support her drug habit. Then the whole truth came out. Through sobs, she told the counselor that she had been renting out her two-year-old daughter to men who wanted her for kinky sex. She made more money renting her child out for an hour than she could make on her own in an entire night. The counselor had never heard anything like that. He didn't know what to say. Finally, he asked her, "Have you thought of going to a church for help?" He later said, "I will never forget the look of pure, naive shock that crossed her face. 'Church!' she cried. 'Why would I ever go there? I was already feeling terrible about myself. They'd just make me feel worse.'"[15]

The sucker punch of that story is that if you study Jesus' life, perhaps the most remarkable thing about him is that he was the only sinless person to ever walk the face of the planet, and yet everywhere he went, the most sinful people were drawn to him like a magnet.

Why?

Because Jesus didn't make people feel worse.

He made them feel loved.

Jesus knew a secret that many Christians today seem to have forgotten: *it's love that turns a life around.* The way to change a life is not by judging people but by embracing them. Not by pointing out their sins but by pointing the way to hope.

What's so disturbing is that what Jesus was known for— amazing grace—is the exact opposite of what Christians are known for today. We're known for judgment and condemnation. We're known not for what we're for—loving God and loving people—but for what we're against.

Jesus spoke truth to people, but he always led with love. That's why sinful people wanted to be around Jesus, and why Jesus was called a "friend of . . . sinners."[16]

One of those sinners was Zacchaeus. Like many of the people gathered around Jesus when he told the three search-and-rescue stories, Zacchaeus was a tax collector. Worse, he was the city of Jericho's *chief* tax collector. More than anyone else in his town, Zacchaeus was responsible for making sure the Roman army—whose soldiers were impaling Jewish men, women, and children on poles—was well funded. Zacchaeus, a Jew, was collecting exorbitant taxes from the other Jews to pay for the Roman army so they could annihilate more Jewish people.

If anyone deserved condemnation from God, it was Zacchaeus. So when Jesus comes to Jericho, does he condemn Zacchaeus? Does Jesus make him feel worse? No, Jesus asks if he can have lunch at Zacchaeus's house.[17]

Jesus loved not only to tell stories but also to *write* stories. We have no evidence that Jesus ever put pen to paper,* but he wrote stories in human lives. He would meet a person, and the interaction would leave the person changed. It was like that person's story was rewritten. And the agent that Jesus used to produce this change in people was love.

That's exactly what happens with Zacchaeus. Jesus poured God's love on him, and it turned his life upside down. Heaven spilled into Zacchaeus that day.

Jesus continues to rewrite people's lives today. My life is one of his many incredible second drafts. My father was a con artist who was in and out of prison. My mother was Jewish by birth, an atheist by choice. I never went to church and had no exposure to Jesus. I grew up sad and tried to bury my feelings in alcohol and drugs, then in success. That's when Jesus entered my life. I know it sounds like I'm telling you some kind of fairy tale, but this one's true. Jesus flipped my

---

*Ink to papyrus?

script. I'll tell you more about that later. But for now, I'll tell you that despite the inauspicious beginning of my story, God has given me the honor of being part of starting two churches trying to follow in the way of Jesus by pouring God's love on all kinds of people. I started a church in Virginia Beach in 1997, where I pastored for twelve years. Then I moved to Las Vegas to start Verve. And Las Vegas is where I met all the prodigals I mentioned earlier. All those prodigals are people who have had their stories rewritten by Jesus.

Peter, the believer in reincarnation, gave his life to Jesus.

Hector, who grew up in a Las Vegas gang, told everyone just before we baptized him, "I spent my entire life in gangs. Walking into this church was the first time I've ever felt accepted for who I am."

Dharma, the topless dancer, came to Verve, discovered that God loves her for what's on the inside, and decided to quit dancing topless.

Randy, the addict who called our church to find out if we had a 12-step program, started coming to our church and found a higher power named Jesus, and Jesus has set him free.

David, who was wanted as a drug dealer in Ohio, gave his life to Christ, and he has totally changed.

The same happened to Julie, the pole-dancing instructor. And Scott and Cooper, the atheists. And the two teenage sons of Frank, the strip-club bouncer. And Sal, the casino pitboss.

After many long conversations at Starbucks, Jack, the alcoholic taxi driver, was baptized in my pool.

Cici, the crystal meth addict who was part of the neo-Nazi, white-supremacist, skinhead hate group, called our church because she had heard about us on a sex website.* She called because she was about to commit suicide. She was persuaded not to, and that Sunday she showed up at our church. Soon, her life inverted. She gave her life to Jesus and then to feeding homeless people. In fact, she got other people from Verve involved, and each Thanksgiving they would feed hundreds of homeless people. I asked Cici what led her to do that, assuming she had probably experienced homelessness at some point in her troubled journey. She told me she had briefly been homeless once, but that wasn't her reason for wanting to help the homeless. What has driven her is that the homeless are the skinheads' biggest targets. They practice killing homeless people because no one misses them when they're gone; the police rarely investigate when one is found beaten to death. And Cici said that now nothing gets to her like seeing homeless people smile when she serves them.

Sandy, the Britney Spears impersonator, showed up at Verve after seeing a card for our church that said, "God for the Rest of Us." And Sandy, who had gone to church a variety of times throughout her life, was shocked to learn that God loved her. That Jesus came to save her, not to condemn her. And Sandy said yes. She dove into God's Kingdom, and everything about her life has changed.**

---

*Apparently we're all the rage on Vegas's sex websites. I think that's as weird as you do. Please don't write me letters.

**If you're wondering, yes, her job has changed too. She's no longer a Britney Spears impersonator.

In fact, what has changed *all those people* is learning that God is for the rest of us. He's not just for the missionary doctors and the Baptists and the preachers. No, he's also for the abortion doctors and the bisexuals and the pornographers.

This is why Jesus came. Not to condemn us for our sins but to save us from them. And to let us know that no matter what we've done, God still loves us.

He is wastefully extravagant with his love. He is for every person who has rejected him in Las Vegas. He was for the tax collectors and sinners who had rejected him by seeking pleasure. He was for the Pharisees and teachers of the law who rejected him through their prideful moralism. And he's for you.

Personally, I've gone from not knowing God at all, to struggling to believe that he could love someone like me, to starting two churches for people who have no interest in a God whom they think has no interest in them. Each step of the way I've been learning more about who God is for. And I'm going to share my story—and what I've learned—with you, because I think it can change your life. And it could change the lives of the people God puts in your path.

Your Story

My guess is your story is kind of similar to the story of either the sinners or the Pharisees who surrounded Jesus that day.

If you're like the "sinners and tax collectors," you have trouble believing God's love is for you, because you think you're too bad. You feel like your immoral life has lowered you to a place beyond the reach of God's grace.

If you're in this group, you're still stuck on the sentence where I said that God is for abortion doctors, bisexuals, and pornographers. And you have a thousand questions you want to ask:

"If God really is for them, maybe God could also be for me?"

"Is it more accurate to say that God would be for me if I stopped doing the things I'm doing?"

"But what about my sin?"

"What if I say yes to God but keep on sinning? The one thing I don't want to be is a hypocrite."

"Don't I have to obey Jesus for him to love me? Are you just nice and trying to make me feel good?"

"Is this the book I've been waiting for, the one that could change my life?"

"Are you ever going to answer these questions or not?"

Yes, I'll answer them. In fact, I think the answers will come out in just about every chapter in this book.

If you're like the Pharisees and teachers of the law, you have trouble believing God's love is for "them" because you think you're so good. You feel like your moral life has raised you to a place where you deserve God's favor.

If you're in this group, you're still stuck on the sentence where I said that God is for abortion doctors, bisexuals, and pornographers. And you have a thousand questions you want to ask:

"Isn't it too strong to say God is *for* them?"

"Maybe it'd be more accurate to say that God *would be*

for them *if* they stopped being abortion doctors, bisexuals, and pornographers?"

"But what about sin? Is this author soft on sin?"

"If we tell those kinds of people God is for them, will they take that as permission to keep on sinning?"

"All those 'prodigals' in Las Vegas, were they told the hard truth about sin and obedience to Jesus as Lord, or did you just give them a cotton-candy version of Christianity that made them feel good?"

"Should I even continue reading this book?"

"Are you ever going to answer these questions or not?"

Yes, I'll answer them, but not yet. I think it may be healthy for you to live in that tension for a while. I might even make you wait till the last chapter.

So my guess is that your story is kind of similar to the story of either the sinners or the Pharisees who surrounded Jesus that day. And if that's true, Jesus wants to change your story. He loves telling stories, and he would love to tell a new story with your life. He loves writing stories, and perhaps there's some rewriting that needs to happen with your personal script.

My hope is that as you read the stories of God's audacious and life-shaping grace in this book, it will start to remold your story.

And the agent of change that Jesus will use in your life is love, the love of a wastefully extravagant God who *is* for the rest of us—and is for *you* as well.

2

GOD FOR THE PROSTITUTES

HAVE YOU EVER EXPERIENCED a time when you were uninvited? Did it leave you feeling unwanted or undesirable?

When I was in first grade, my father believed he was wanted by the FBI. We lived on the run and in fear. I had a fake last name. For now I'm going to keep you in the dark about the details, just like everyone at my school was. At school I seemed like a normal kid. I was pretty popular—no surprise. But the shocker is . . . I was not the *most* popular boy in my class. His name was Tommy Gardener. Why was Tommy Gardener more popular than I was? I just don't know.*

---

*I assume the girls thought he could supply them with vegetables and flowers.

There was this girl in our class named Amy. For her birthday, Amy had a sleepover party. She invited all the girls in our class . . . and Tommy Gardener!

He came over to me. "Are you invited to Amy's sleepover party?"

"No." I was confused. "Are *you* invited to Amy's sleepover party?"

Tommy smiled. "Yes."

Now at this point you have to ask: What kind of girl invites a boy to a sleepover party? I don't know. It certainly makes you wonder about her character and moral purity. But she did. She invited him.

And Tommy Gardener accepted the invitation!

What kind of boy would want to go to a girls' sleepover?

I don't know . . . but I wanted to go too!

But I couldn't because I was uninvited.

So many people have come to a point where they believe that *if* there is a God, *if* he's offering relationship, *if* he brings some people to heaven when they die, he wouldn't do these things for them. They believe his attitude toward them would be, in the words of Alanis Morissette, "But you, you're not allowed; you're uninvited."

Perhaps you feel that way because you've walked away from God or because of things you've done. You assume you don't meet the standard of moral purity that must be necessary to gain the approval of a perfect God.

If you feel that way, I have really good news for you.

Pharisees and Prostitutes

About two thousand years ago, Jesus walked the earth, claiming to be God. People weren't sure whether to believe that or not. But they assumed that if he was God, he would be for the Pharisees. The Pharisees were the religious leaders at the time, and they taught everyone that God was for *them*. God, they declared, was for people who lived sinless lives, and they—the Pharisees—lived sinless lives. Or so they claimed. The truth is, they were *not* sinless, but they liked to think they were; the expression "holier than thou" could have been invented to describe the Pharisees. They said that to be acceptable to God, you had to follow the rules, follow the religious traditions, follow the Pharisees' ritualistic ordinances for purity, *and* keep yourself separate from anyone who was impure or sinful.

And it quickly became obvious that there was a problem. Jesus was hanging out with *prostitutes*. Now, there were never accusations of sexual impropriety. But Jesus *was* a friend of prostitutes, and prostitutes wanted to be friends with Jesus. If the Pharisees were right, it should have been something Jesus was ashamed of, that he hid from others. But Jesus didn't hide it. In fact, he kind of shoved it in the Pharisees' faces. For example, one time Jesus said to some of the religious leaders, "Truly I tell you, the tax collectors and the prostitutes are entering the kingdom of God ahead of you. For John came to you to show you the way of righteousness, and you did not believe him, but the tax collectors and the prostitutes did. And even after you saw this, you did not repent and believe him."[1]

And so some people started to think, "Wow. Jesus is a friend of prostitutes. So . . . I guess he's *not* God? Because we know God is *not* for the prostitutes. The Pharisees taught us that."

The whole situation came to a head one night at a Pharisee's house. "When one of the Pharisees invited Jesus to have dinner with him, he went to the Pharisee's house and reclined at the table."[2] So this dinner party had a bunch of Pharisees . . . and Jesus. Before dinner, everyone would have gone through a ritualistic cleansing, as they did before every meal, making sure they were purified from anything that might have defiled them from their time out in the world that day.

As you read this story, don't imagine a dinner party you might attend today. Back then, this type of dinner party would have involved hours of discussing deep issues like politics, social trends, and theology.

The meal would take place in an outer room of the house, and there would typically be a porch circling this outer room. The door of the house would be left open so people from the town could come and sit on the porch to listen to the conversation. They didn't have radio or Internet or TV back then, so people weren't sitting home watching *The Real Housewives of Jerusalem*. Listening to the dinner conversations of important people was their entertainment.

It was typical for the Pharisees to gather for a meal to talk about God and theology, and the crowd who would typically gather to listen were those who aligned themselves with the Pharisees and were therefore interested in what they had to say.

But on this night Jesus was also at the table. And although he, like the Pharisees, claimed to represent God, he had a different sort of fan base. Garth Brooks might say that Jesus had friends in low places.

In fact, one of the ways the Pharisees would put Jesus down was by nicknaming him the "friend of sinners." But Jesus didn't take it as an insult. He would smile and explain that's why he came. He came for people who were far from God, who had messed up, who were down and out, who were broken and in need of healing. He would tell those people that God was for them.

And so out on the porch that night, listening in on the dinner conversation, in addition to the self-righteous fans of the Pharisees, there was probably a group of sinful fans of Jesus.

What happened next shocked everyone. "A woman in that town who lived a sinful life learned that Jesus was eating at the Pharisee's house, so she came there with an alabaster jar of perfume."[3] The words "a woman in that town who lived a sinful life" were almost certainly code for "the town prostitute."

And she was uninvited, not only to this party, but to every respectable place she went, because of her lack of character and moral purity. Because she was the kind of girl who invited boys over for sleepovers.

So the town prostitute learned that Jesus was eating at the Pharisee's house, and she showed up uninvited, walking up onto the crowded porch. Everyone on the porch knew who she was, so they were thinking, *What is she doing here?*

But she walked right through the crowd and into the house without saying a word.

Shocking.

From the perspective of the Pharisees, this despised woman entering the room would have destroyed the ritual purity they had established for the evening.

And she would have known how they viewed her. But it didn't matter. She couldn't help herself.

"As she stood behind [Jesus] at his feet weeping, she began to wet his feet with her tears. Then she wiped them with her hair, kissed them and poured perfume on them."[4]

She walked in carrying what was probably the most precious thing she owned. An alabaster jar of perfume would have been a prized possession for a woman back then. This wasn't your daily perfume. It was like a savings account. It could be used only once. This had been her treasure, but something had changed. Jesus was now her treasure. And to demonstrate that, she walked up to Jesus, broke the jar open, and poured the contents out on Jesus' feet.

Realizing that Jesus' feet were now wet from the perfume and from her tears, she wanted to dry them. Not having a towel, she let down her hair and started using it to wipe his feet. At that time, Jewish women did not unbind their hair in public. To do so was considered scandalous, almost pornographic, in their culture. But this woman seemingly had a complete disregard for the opinions of anyone in that room, except for Jesus. Her focus was only on Jesus.

And in that moment, *everyone's* focus was on Jesus. What

would he do? The Pharisee's focus was *definitely* on Jesus. In fact, we're told what the host Pharisee was thinking. "When the Pharisee who had invited him saw this, he said to himself, 'If this man were a prophet, he would know who is touching him and what kind of woman she is—that she is a sinner.'"[5]

The Pharisee assumed Jesus didn't realize this woman was a prostitute. Thus Jesus must not be God, as he claimed, or even a prophet. Because if he were, he would know who the woman was, and he wouldn't allow her to be near him. After all, according to the Pharisees, godly people, religious people, sinless people don't hang around sinners; they would certainly never allow themselves to be touched by a sinner.[*] Basically this guy was thinking, *Jesus, you are not who you claim to be, are you?*

And I love how Jesus responded. Because the Pharisee was thinking, *You don't know people the way someone sent by God would know people.* And Jesus basically said, "Oh yeah? Well, I know *you*. In fact, I just read your mind. Let me show you. . . ."

Jesus answered him, "Simon, I have something to tell you."

"Tell me, teacher," he said.

---

[*]It's interesting that Jesus didn't cringe at the inappropriate behavior of lost people. All the righteous Pharisees were offended by the salaciousness not only of the woman's life choices but also of her actions in this moment. Jesus was not. He looked past her choices and actions and saw a woman made in the image of God and in desperate need of her heavenly Father. What's sad is that Christians today follow the Pharisees' lead and blanch at sin rather than, like Jesus, looking past the sin and embracing the person.

"Two people owed money to a certain money-lender. One owed him five hundred denarii, and the other fifty. Neither of them had the money to pay him back, so he forgave the debts of both. Now which of them will love him more?"

Simon replied, "I suppose the one who had the bigger debt forgiven."

"You have judged correctly," Jesus said.

Then he turned toward the woman and said to Simon, "Do you see this woman? I came into your house. You did not give me any water for my feet, but she wet my feet with her tears and wiped them with her hair. You did not give me a kiss, but this woman, from the time I entered, has not stopped kissing my feet. You did not put oil on my head, but she has poured perfume on my feet. Therefore, I tell you, her many sins have been forgiven—as her great love has shown. But whoever has been forgiven little loves little."

Then Jesus said to her, "Your sins are forgiven."

The other guests began to say among themselves, "Who is this who even forgives sins?"[6]

They asked that because they knew that only God can forgive sins. So when Jesus said, "Your sins are forgiven," he was claiming to be God.

Then Jesus said to the woman, "Your faith has saved you; go in peace."[7] What a story.

And reading it, you've got to ask: Why did this woman come and do this?

Well, Jesus said it's because she had been forgiven much. She couldn't help but express her gratitude.

Apparently, this woman—maybe earlier that day or the day before—had met Jesus, had heard him speak, had listened to his message of love and forgiveness.

It makes me curious. I wonder what she heard Jesus say. Luke, who shares this story, doesn't tell us what Jesus was teaching in that town that day.

But we might be able to figure it out. Earlier in Luke's account, we're told that some disciples of John the Baptist[*] had shown up to ask Jesus whether he really was the Messiah.

And in chapter eleven of Matthew (one of the other Gospels[**]) we also read about that incident when John the Baptist's disciples came to Jesus. And Matthew *does* tell us what Jesus was preaching that day.

Imagine this woman, the town prostitute, standing in the back of the crowd, looking at Jesus, listening to Jesus, this man who claimed to represent God, a man who was obviously so different from any man she had ever met. And then he speaks and says, "Come to me, all you who are weary and burdened, and I will give you rest. Take my yoke upon you and learn from me, for I am gentle and humble in heart, and you will find rest for your souls."[8]

Can you imagine how that sounded to her?

---

[*] Another spiritual leader of the time.
[**] The other books in the Bible that document the life of Jesus.

How might that invitation sound to you? How might it impact your life, if you were to take Jesus up on it?

Who knows how she had gotten where she was, what had happened to her? The vast majority of women in the sex industry today were abused as children, often sexually. Maybe that was her story. I don't know. I don't know how she got there, but she had grown up into a life of condemnation—being condemned by others and, I would assume, condemning herself.

I can't imagine that she grew up hoping to become a prostitute. No little girl grows up dreaming about that. Children don't grow up planning on being ashamed of themselves, of their sin. They just end up there. As she had.

And she thought she would always stay that way. She would always be uninvited, unwanted, undesirable—except by men who just wanted to use her. Who would help her out of this life? The only response she received from anyone was condemnation, and that didn't change her. Pointing out her sins didn't lead her away from her sins. Shame didn't set her free. So she thought this was her life, and it would always be her life.

But here was Jesus, who claimed to be God, and he said, "Come to me. Be yoked to me."

A yoke was a device that connected two animals together. So Jesus was essentially saying, "I want a connected relationship with you. I am gentle and humble in heart. I won't condemn you. I'm offering you *forgiveness*. And I can set you free. You are not defined by your sin. You are not captive to your sin. You can be free. I can give your soul what it needs—rest. And I can give you new life."

In that moment, the woman realized it didn't matter who she was, what she had done, what anyone else thought of her. *God* was for her. She was invited. And she said *yes*. She accepted that forgiveness.

Later, she heard that Jesus was a dinner guest at Simon the Pharisee's house, and so she grabbed her most valued treasure and headed over. She walked in, and this broken woman broke her jar, perhaps symbolizing that her life—which is truly a person's most treasured possession—had been broken but was now being put back together, made whole.

And Jesus explained to Simon that the reason she did it was gratitude, because she had been forgiven much. Jesus made the point that Simon, who falsely felt superior and who falsely considered himself sinless, didn't feel a need to be forgiven, so he wouldn't understand an extravagant act of love like this.

To make sure no one missed the point, Jesus turned to the woman, smiled at her, and said, "Your sins are forgiven."[9]

"Your faith has saved you; go in peace."[10]

Can you imagine what went through people's minds as they heard Jesus say all this? Out on the porch, shock waves must have gone through the crowd, because inside were the Pharisees and a prostitute, and it was obvious that Jesus was *for* the prostitute. What they heard was Jesus basically saying that God was for the *prostitutes*, *not* the Pharisees.

And in the house was the prostitute—broken pieces of

the jar on the floor all around her, still unable to stop crying, using her hair as a ShamWow to dry Jesus' feet—and what *she* heard was that her broken life was being made whole.

Jesus was offering her new life. No longer a life of condemnation, but a life of peace. Peace with other people, peace with herself, and (most important) peace with God.

It's a beautiful story.

You and Me and Them

It's not only a beautiful story, it's a *relevant* story. It's relevant to you and me. Now, you may question that, because you're probably not a prostitute.

Or are you?

Back in the Old Testament there was this godly man named Hosea. He was single, and as most single people do, he had probably prayed that God would give him a perfect wife.

One day God speaks and tells Hosea he's picked a girl for him. The bad news is that her name is Gomer. The worse news is that she's a prostitute.

Hosea is confused. But God insists. And Hosea obeys. He goes down to the red-light district and pays Gomer's pimp so he can take her home as his wife.

Surprisingly, things seem to go well. Hosea actually ends up falling in love with Gomer. He gives his heart to her. But one day Gomer disappears. And Hosea learns the heartbreaking news: she's gone back to turning tricks.

What do those men offer her that I don't? Hosea must have

wondered. *Why would she turn away from me for them?* And Hosea looks to the heavens and asks, "What now, God?"

And God speaks to Hosea again. He tells him to go find Gomer, buy her from her pimp for the second time, and bring her home so Hosea can love her again as his wife. Hosea is confused. He demands to know why. And God says, "Because that's how I love *you*."[11]

God uses Hosea as a living object lesson. Hosea represents God, and Gomer represents, well, *us*.

We're the prostitutes.

We've all turned our backs on God and looked in all kinds of other places for the love that only he can give us.

The lesson is that even if you've turned away from God, even if you've done so repeatedly, even if you've been far from perfect, God's love for you is still perfect.

And even if you've been against God, he's still for you. And you're still invited.

Now some people really struggle to accept the idea that God could love them. Maybe you find it difficult to believe that a perfect God could love an imperfect person like you. I understand that. I think Gomer would understand that. I wonder if the reason she left Hosea and went back to her old life is because she could never fully believe he loved her.

The prostitute who came and crashed the Pharisee's party would understand that. But when she met Jesus, everything changed.

When *I* met Jesus, everything changed.

My prayer for you is that *you'll* meet Jesus and you'll hear him say to you, "Come to me, all you who are weary and burdened, and I will give you rest. Take my yoke upon you and learn from me, for I am gentle and humble in heart, and you will find rest for your souls." Because if you really heard those words, everything would change for you. You'd realize you are loved much, you can be forgiven much, and it will lead you to love him much. You'd understand that God is for you and you're invited. So you can go to God in peace.

I told you how I was uninvited to Amy's first-grade sleepover birthday party. She invited only one boy, and it was Tommy Gardener.

I wanted to be un-uninvited. I wanted *in*. So I wrote Amy a letter. It went like this:

Dear Amy: Heard about your party. I was talking to Tommy. He's glad you invited him, but he's the only boy invited and, well, that's kind of weird for him. Ya know, being the ONLY boy . . . since you invited only *one* boy. Anyway, just thought you'd want to know.

Amy wrote me a note back. It said, "Okay, you're invited."

Yes! Never underestimate the power of manipulation, especially on unsuspecting first-grade girls with questionable moral character.

The good news is you don't need to manipulate God into wanting you.

You don't need to convince him that you're acceptable.

You don't have to beg him to invite you, because . . . you're already invited.

All you have to do is realize God is for you, and say yes.

Once you understand that you're unfaithful and an adulterer in God's eyes, but he loves and invites you anyway, and you say yes, the passion of your life becomes letting other people know that they're invited too.

That passion led me to start a church in the heart of Sin City for sinners who didn't think God was for them.

One night I was in Orlando at a banquet for church planters. When it ended, a friend came over and told me that someone was asking who I was. He took me over to meet this guy. Dude said his name was Jeff. He was a church planter but also a professional chef. He had heard about me through a friend we had in common. He had recently come to Las Vegas to meet with a wealthy business owner who didn't know Jeff was a pastor. In the middle of their meeting, Jeff decided to mention that he was a pastor, hoping to start a spiritual conversation. But when he said "pastor," the business owner exclaimed, "I hate church!"

"Oh," Jeff said, "I'm sorry. Why do you hate church?"

"I've always hated church," the man explained with disgust, "but now I have a brand-new reason."

"Why is that?" Jeff asked.

"Because," the rich businessman said, "I love prostitutes."

Jeff realized this was not a typical conversation. "Why does your loving prostitutes make you hate church?"

"Because my favorite prostitute started going to some

41

church"—he frowned—"and they told her God loves her, so she decided to stop being a prostitute. She totally changed her life, left Vegas, and moved back home to start a new life. I hate church!"

Jeff smiled. "Do you happen to know what church it was?" he asked.

"Yeah," the business man said, "she kept telling me I should go to it. It's called Verve. The pastor's name is Vince Antonucci."

"Oh," Jeff said with some surprise, "one of my friends is a good friend of Vince Antonucci."

The business owner said, "I hate that guy."

He may hate me, but God loves me.

And God loves that businessman's favorite prostitute. And someone had to let her know. I'm so grateful that God used me to do that.

Learning that God was for her changed her life.

I'm sure she had been condemned. Maybe even had someone point a finger at her and call her a sinner. (Like she didn't already know that.) But condemnation didn't turn her life around.

Love did.

And when you realize God loves you, you need to share that love with others.

Who can you let know that they're invited?

3

GOD FOR THE SHAME FILLED

I'm about to let you in on my secret.

The battle of my life is with shame. It's the ghost that haunts me. I can run, hide, try to distract myself, but it always finds a way of making its ugly presence known.

That should not be a secret. The problem is when you're filled with shame, it somehow feels shameful to let others know.

Are you haunted by shame?

What is shame? It's not guilt. Guilt is feeling bad about doing something wrong. Shame is feeling that *you* are bad. It's a generic feeling, not attached to anything you've done.

Guilt is feeling convicted that I've made a mistake. Shame is being convinced that *I am* a mistake.

Guilt is actually a positive thing. It leads us to confess, to repent, to change our behavior. But there's nothing positive about shame. Shame says you are a negative, and since it's generic, there's no behavior to confess, repent, or change.

Guilt is brought on us by the choices we make. Shame is painted on us by the people we listen to.

It haunts the girl who grew up being molested by her uncle and to this day has a sense of being dirty.

It plagues the boy whose father told him repeatedly that he'd never amount to much. Eventually it got tattooed on his soul. And today he feels like a man who hasn't amounted to much.

It follows the girl who grew up being told by her mother that she needed to lose weight because boys don't like heavy girls. So her whole life she's kept guys who showed interest in her at arm's length because she knows they'll ultimately reject her. Her mother told her so.

I grew up with a harsh father who refused to show affection. He never said the words "I love you." What he did communicate was that I was unworthy, that I was unbearable, and that I was too stupid to say or do anything intelligent. I lived my childhood in fear of his disapproval. And early on, I became convinced that he was right about me. It's not like I had a lot of other opinions to go on. And he was my father. He was the role model, authority figure, and life shaper I had been given. So his opinion of me formed *my* opinion of me. In fact, to this day, I become suspicious when someone shows me affection or gives me a compliment, because I know they must be lying. I'm obviously not worthy of love or capable of doing anything deserving praise.

Why? What have I done to warrant my self-loathing? I don't know. Nothing, really. It's just a generic feeling I have about myself.

That's shame.

The way my father looked at me led me to a place where I didn't want to be looked at. I wanted to be alone and unnoticed. Being a burden to my dad led me to not want to exist at all. Growing up, I constantly thought death was preferable to life, and on several occasions I made halfhearted attempts at suicide. When I failed, it only confirmed what my father thought about me. He was right; I couldn't even succeed at killing myself.

That's shame.

So how do you get past your shame? How can *I* get past my shame?

That's something I've been struggling with for years. Recently I bought the book *I Thought It Was Just Me* by Brené Brown, who is a leading expert on shame. As I read how she defined shame and explained how to get past it, I was taken back to a story in the Bible. And I realized that about two thousand years before Brown shared brilliant insights about the journey out of shame, Jesus was putting those principles into practice.

Untouchable

She was a broken woman.

Her body was broken. She had been bleeding nonstop for twelve years.[1] We're not told exactly, but it seems she had a chronic menstrual disorder.*

Such a condition would be onerous for any woman of any era, but for a Jewish woman of that time, in that culture, the burden was far more oppressive. She would have been considered untouchable. According to the law, anyone she touched or who touched her would have been made "unclean."[2] If she was married, her husband could not touch her. Her condition would have left her unable to bear children. And if she'd had a child prior to her twelve-year nightmare, that child could not touch her. Not only that, but she would not be allowed to enter the Temple to worship God. I've heard this woman described as "walking pollution." That's how everyone would have viewed her.

And so, she was a broken woman.

But it wasn't just her body that was broken. It was much worse. It was her soul. It only makes sense that her condition would have left her drowning in shame, and in her thinking and her actions we see telltale signs that she was shame filled.

Brené Brown writes, "Shame is the intensely painful feeling or experience of believing we are flawed and therefore unworthy of acceptance and belonging."[3] With her physical

---

*It's interesting that in the Bible, blood is often a symbol of life. In this case it was not symbolic—the woman was literally losing blood—but I bet the symbolism applied as well. She probably felt like the life was draining out of her.

condition and its social and even spiritual consequences, how could she not feel that way?

Brown continues, "Shame is about the fear of disconnection. When we are experiencing shame, we are steeped in the fear of being ridiculed, diminished or seen as flawed. We are afraid that we've exposed or revealed a part of us that jeopardizes our connection and our worthiness of acceptance."[4] For this woman it wasn't just a fear; it was her reality. God made her in his image, which meant she was designed to live in community. But her condition had ripped apart all of her relational connectedness.

Jean Baker Miller and Irene Pierce Stiver, also specialists in shame research, write,

> "We believe that the most terrifying and destructive feeling that a person can experience is psychological isolation. This is not the same as being alone. It is a feeling that one is locked out of the possibility of human connection and of being powerless to change the situation. In the extreme, psychological isolation can lead to a sense of hopelessness and desperation. People will do almost anything to escape this combination of condemned isolation and powerlessness."[5]

Miller and Stiver perfectly describe this woman in the Bible. She *was* desperate. Not to heal her soul but to heal her body. She viewed her body as the enemy, and we're told that "she had suffered a great deal under the care of many doctors and had spent all she had, yet instead of getting better she grew worse."[6] Her desperation had led her to try everything, but everything had produced nothing. And she was left hopeless. She had been hopeless for a long time.

But then she heard rumors. Whispers of a man named Jesus. Stories that this Jesus had power—healing power. People asked him for healing; he touched them; they were healed. Suddenly she went from being hopeless to having one last hope. Her hope's name was Jesus.

There were still problems. *Lots* of problems. He might never come to her town. If he did, she knew she couldn't approach him. She was unclean. He would look at her and turn away in disgust. And he certainly couldn't touch her. If he did, it would make him unclean.

She came up with a plan. She would approach him from behind—that way he wouldn't know. She wouldn't touch him, just his clothes. Perhaps there would be healing in his garment.

And now all she could do was wait. Until finally, the day arrived. Word spread that Jesus was coming across the lake. She went down to implement her strategy, and there she encountered a problem she hadn't accounted for: a huge crowd of people surrounded Jesus. The problem was that she wasn't allowed to be around people. She couldn't just sneak up behind Jesus, because to do so, she'd have to make her way through the crowd. To make her way through the crowd, she'd have to touch countless people. And every one of those people would then be considered unclean.

But she had to.

Jesus was her last hope.

I wonder how long she stood staring at the crowd from a distance.

I wonder how many times she tried to see the face of Jesus through the horde of humanity surrounding him.

And I wonder how much time it took for her to muster up the courage to make her way through that crowd and get to Jesus.

We don't know. But we read that she made the decision to go for it with the thought, "If I just touch his clothes, I will be healed."[7] What's interesting is that the verb tense in the original language reveals that she was thinking this thought over and over and over. With each step she took toward and then through the crowd, she was still convincing herself; she was still summoning up the grit to move her feet forward.

Finally she got to Jesus, reached out, and touched his cloak. "Immediately her bleeding stopped and she felt in her body that she was freed from her suffering."[8]

She was physically healed.*

But there was a problem. She was focused exclusively on her body, but what she almost certainly didn't understand was that something much deeper inside of her was broken.

Shame is like that. When you struggle with shame, you don't realize you struggle with shame. You don't think, *The*

---

*What happened is amazing. The woman touched Jesus and, in a sense, they traded places. She couldn't stop bleeding. Soon Jesus would go to a cross where he wouldn't be able to stop bleeding. She was sick. On the cross, Jesus took on her sickness—and mine, and yours. And by his wounds, we can all be healed.

reason I feel like I'm a mistake who is unlovable and a burden on the world is because I struggle with shame. No, you just *feel* like a mistake who is unlovable and a burden on the world. That's not an assessment of yourself, given to you or possessed by you. It's just who you are. It's how you look at yourself, and you never realize you're looking at yourself through shame-colored glasses.

This woman thought she was totally better because her body had been healed. But shame was her primary problem. That's why she was the only person in the Bible who ever snuck up on Jesus for a covert healing. That's why, *after* being healed physically, rather than thanking Jesus, she tried to slink off through the crowd. Think about that. She had been physically healed. She was no longer unclean. Why try to get away unnoticed? You would think she had nothing more to hide, nothing more to keep her distant from others. But actually, she did. Her shame.

Brené Brown writes,

"Shame often prevents us from presenting our real selves to the people around us—it sabotages our efforts to be authentic. . . . We *cannot* share ourselves with others when we see ourselves as flawed and unworthy of connection. It's impossible to be 'real' when we are ashamed of who we are or what we believe."[9]

In his book *Scary Close*, Donald Miller shares how a counselor helped him to understand shame. Picture a circle on a piece of paper. That circle represents you. It's the real you. It's the you you're supposed to be. But there's a problem, which is represented by a circle around your circle. The problem is that someone made you feel like the real you isn't good enough or isn't worth loving. That feeling, which encircles and engulfs the real you, is shame. Shame leaves you convinced that people won't accept the real you. So you don't want them to see the real you. But you don't want people to see your shame, either. So what you do is create a false self you show the world. This false self is represented by a circle around the circle of shame, which is around the circle symbolizing the real you. This outermost circle is who you show to other people to try to gain their approval. For you, it might be that you make sure everyone knows you're smart. Or maybe you hide behind being funny, the class clown. Or you might be trying to show the world how successful you are. Or you might be the girl who boys can have their way with; at least that way, they'll want you.

When we live in shame, we create a false self to show the world. If we can't do that, we try not to let the world see us at all, which is what the woman who touched Jesus did. She got to Jesus, touched him, was physically healed, and started to sneak away.

And then Jesus spoke: "Who touched me?"

His disciples looked at the swarm of people all pressing in to be close to him and responded as we probably would: "Duh." They were like, "Um, I think *everyone* has touched you, Jesus. We didn't realize you were so touchy about being touched, but if you are, hanging out in the middle of mob scenes may not be your thing."

But Jesus was like, "Don't *duh* me." He wouldn't back down. He "kept looking around to see who had done it."[10]

Why did Jesus insist on discovering who had touched him? Obviously this woman didn't want to be pointed out. She had been embarrassed enough in her life and thought being singled out in front of this huge crowd would just pile more embarrassment on her. So why did Jesus insist on discovering who had touched him?

Because he already knew who had touched him. And he knew that her issue went deeper, that she needed to come forward.

Brown writes,

> There is nothing more frustrating, and sometimes frightening, than feeling pain and not being able to describe it or explain it to someone. It doesn't matter if it's physical pain or emotional pain. When we can't find the right words to explain our painful experiences to others, we often feel alone and scared. Some of us may even feel anger or rage and act out. Eventually, many of us shut down and either live silently with the pain or, in cases where we can't, accept someone else's definition of what we are feeling simply out of the desperate need to find some remedy.[11]

Jesus knew if the woman snuck off thinking she was all better, she would have quickly discovered something was still wrong, because she still would have *felt* wrong. Touching Jesus' garment had healed her body, but it was empathy that would heal her shame-torn soul. As Brown explains, "*empathy* is the strongest antidote for shame."[12]

And so Jesus stirred up the crowd, searching for this unknown person who had touched him, and finally the woman felt forced to come forward. She "came and fell at his feet and, trembling with fear, told him the whole truth."[13] Researchers tell us that part of the path out of shame is to "speak our shame." We have to get to a place where we give words to our pain and share our stories with others.

And that's exactly what Jesus forced this woman to do. And the moment she finished sharing "the whole truth" became the most important moment of her life. For her, time probably stood still. She had confessed all the ugliness of her life not only to this man who claimed to God in human flesh but to a mass of people. What would happen next? How would Jesus respond?

He responded by calling her "Daughter."

He said, "Daughter, your faith has healed you. Go in peace and be freed from your suffering."[14] This is the only recorded time Jesus called anyone "daughter." Can you imagine how it made her feel when Jesus looked her in the eyes and called her by that tender term of endearment? When was the last time a man had said anything to her? When was the last time anyone had spoken to her with affection?

God, come down to earth, called her "daughter." He let

her know that despite how she was made to feel about herself, she was his child. That who she was, viewed without the shame-colored glasses, was a beloved child of God.

Moments earlier the touch of Jesus had healed her body. Now the empathy of Jesus flooded and healed her soul.

Brown writes, "Empathy, the most powerful tool of compassion, is an emotional skill that allows us to respond to others in a meaningful, caring way. . . . When we share a difficult experience with someone, and that person responds in an open, deeply connected way—that's empathy."[15] She goes so far as to say, "Empathy creates a hostile environment for shame—it can't survive."[16]

Shame isolates us, and we can't be healed of shame in isolation. "We heal through our connection with others."[17]

This woman had just enough courage to get herself to Jesus and to touch him. And it healed her body. What she didn't understand is that God is for the shame filled. She didn't have enough courage to share her story with Jesus, but Jesus pulled it out of her. And his response healed her and gave her a new self-identity.

She wasn't untouchable.

She was "daughter."

Instantly?

What I'm finding is that my story has a lot in common with the story of the woman who touched Jesus' garment that day, with one possible exception.

Like her, I came to a place in my life where I felt untouchable. Like there was something wrong with me, and I would contaminate anyone I came in contact with.

Like her, I felt isolated and unable to connect with others.

Like her, one day I saw Jesus from a distance.

Like her, I found myself in a place where Jesus forced me to have an encounter with him and left me with a choice of whether I would become vulnerable with him.

Like her, in desperation I decided it was something I had to do.

And like her, I realized that Jesus changed everything for me. My father never showed me he loved me. But through Jesus, my heavenly Father did. He called me his son. And his love, which is the most powerful healing force in the universe, came flooding into my soul.

Here's the possible exception: in the Bible we're told that the woman's bleeding stopped and she experienced physical healing immediately. What we don't know is whether her shame-scarred soul healed immediately as well.

Mine didn't.

It *is* healing. Every day, day after day, I'm better able to look at myself through God's eyes rather than my dad's eyes. More than ever I'm able to feel a sense of God's approval, rather than having it always drowned out by the echoes of my father's disapproval. Increasingly, I'm able to accept affection from others.

But I'm not completely healed yet. It's been a difficult journey, and it's one I'm still on.

My guess is that the process for that woman was similar.

That she would still catch herself thinking she was unclean. That she couldn't help but wonder if women in the market turned away because she wasn't worth saying hello to. That for a long time she flinched a bit whenever someone touched her.

We don't know how immediate it was, but we *do* know that Jesus brought her healing.

And think about this: What if he hadn't? What if he had let her touch his cloak and walk away? What if he hadn't made her stop? What if he hadn't led her to tell her story? What if he had never spoken to her? She would have stopped bleeding, but she would still have thought of herself as unclean as she continued to live in isolation and sneak through crowds.

But because Jesus *did*, her story was forever changed.

The Shame Filled among Us

We don't really know the rest of that woman's story, but the story I find myself wondering about is *yours*. Is it possible that something happened to you that led you to be filled with shame? Is it possible that you've been looking at yourself through shame-colored glasses but just never knew it? Has it left you feeling like a mistake or struggling to connect deeply with other people? You need to understand that you have a God who is for the shame filled. And you need to speak your shame to him and then listen as Jesus speaks to you. And what he'll call you is . . . daughter, son. He knows you, the real you, and he loves you. He thinks you're worthwhile. In fact, he thinks you're worth dying for.

Because of him, you can feel safe in life. Repeatedly in the Bible, God tells us he wants to be our refuge, our safe place.[18] This world can be a scary place, and you don't know if you'll be loved for who you are, and you don't know if you'll be accepted. But instead of hiding behind a false self, just be your real self and take refuge in God's love for you.

As you stop hiding behind a false self and start being real (because you know the real you is accepted by God), you'll be able to connect with people in a deeper way. And that will help you even more to heal from your shame, because we heal through connection with others.

And other people can heal through connection with you. Think about the people God has put into your life. How many do you know who are drowning in shame and don't know that there's a cloak they can reach out and touch? You need to reach out to them. And you need to let them know that there is a God who is for them and who can heal the shame filled. A God who loves them so much he came for them and went to a cross, where he bore their shame so they wouldn't have to anymore.

4

GOD FOR THE ADDICTS

MOST PEOPLE IN REHAB get letters from family and friends
back home. Those letters encourage them to stick with it
and give them hope that they can change. Scott sat in rehab,
reading the letter he had just received from home. It told him
he had to leave rehab because there was no hope for him. It
wasn't that he had done anything wrong in rehab. It was what
he had done before rehab. And he had done a lot.

I met Scott almost four years ago. I had spoken at a church
in Utah, and someone called him. "Scott, you need to check
this guy out. Sounds like his dad was a lot like you." Soon
Scott and I were sitting in a coffee shop on the Las Vegas
Strip. He started unloading his story, and I felt like I was
listening to someone describe my childhood.

Addicted and on the Run

My father was addicted to gambling.

And he never had a job.

Gambling was how he made money. Or, more often and more accurately, how he *lost* money.

Since he had no job, he didn't typically have his own money to lose, so he lost *other* people's money.

He was very charismatic and could charm the wallet right out of someone's pocket. He would show magic tricks to his victims and somehow convince them that his ability to guess what card they were holding meant he could win money for them in a Las Vegas casino.

It might be the neighbors, or other parents from my soccer team, or some celebrity or professional athlete he met.

Occasionally my father would sucker total strangers into going to Vegas with him and funding his gambling venture. These people would cash in their life's savings for chips and sit down at a table with him. Eventually they would leave the table to go to the bathroom, and my father would grab all the chips, cash them in, and race out of the casino before they could find him.

My father almost always had someone after him.

Our family was usually on the run.

One night when I was about six, I woke up to a crash downstairs. I ran down to find the glass from our living room picture window all over the floor and a big brick in the middle of the room. My father grabbed the brick before I could read what was written on it. I asked what had happened, and he told me, "I started collecting bricks!" Yeah.

I think we moved the next day.

Another night when I was maybe nine, there was a knock on the front door. I opened it and saw my Little League coach. This was a fun surprise. But then he asked to talk to my dad. I wondered what this could mean. Had I not been hitting well enough? Was he going to switch the position I played? Why did he need to come to my house and talk to my father about it? The next thing I knew, he and my dad were in the front yard in a fistfight, with my coach yelling that his family was ruined.

I think we moved the next day.

When we weren't moving, my father was rarely home. We lived on the East Coast, and he spent his time in Las Vegas. We had no idea when, or if, he'd come home. But he had a way of keeping us updated. He was convinced that our phones were tapped (he had believed the FBI was after him since before I was born), so he couldn't just call and tell us. Instead, we had a code. He would call collect. We would answer and the operator would say, "I have a collect call from . . ." The name it was from was the first part of the code. I can't remember the details, but it was something like this: "from Vince" meant things were okay, and "from Nick" meant they weren't. The operator would say, "I have a collect call from"—Vince or Nick—and then she would say, "for . . ." The name the call was for was the second part of the code. If he said "Ginger," it meant we needed to pick him up at the airport. If he said

"Ethel," it meant he wasn't coming home. We would then tell the operator, "I'm sorry, she's not here." She would tell my dad, "Caller, your party isn't there. Can I leave a message?" And he would say, "Yes. Please let her know I'll try again tomorrow at 7:30 p.m." or, "Yes. Please let her know I won't be able to call again until next week." That was the third part of the code. If the call was for Ginger and he said he'd try again at 7:30 p.m. the next day, that was when we were to pick him up at the airport. If the call was for Ethel and he couldn't call again till next week, that was when we'd hear from him again, or when he thought he might be able to come home.

A couple of times we picked him up at the airport, excited that he was finally home, only to be told we were moving. That we had to rush back to our house, grab our stuff, and leave immediately.

Once, when I was almost eleven, my father went out to Vegas again, but this time he *didn't* call. No phone ringing. No secret code. No late-night pickup at the airport. Nothing. He didn't come back. So finally, we moved without him.

After that he would repeatedly come in and out of my life, each time with a new wife or girlfriend whose life he would soon destroy.

And after *that*, he was repeatedly in and out of jail.

When I was in college, he wooed the famous baseball player Ted Williams into going into business with him. It wasn't long before he stole money from Teddy Ballgame. Of course he did; he took money from *everyone*. He had to fund his addiction. He got arrested. He went to prison. And then he got out on parole. I never heard from him.

In 1995, I was finishing a ministry internship in Kentucky, and the next week I'd be moving to join the staff of a church outside Washington, DC. My phone rang. It was the pastor of the church I was about to join. He asked if I was watching *America's Most Wanted*. I told him that just because I'd been living in Kentucky for a year, he didn't have to assume I watched *America's Most Wanted* or *Cops*. I also wasn't playing a banjo or drinking moonshine.

He told me I should turn on the show. My father was on it. I asked him if I still had a job.*

His picture was shown on *America's Most Wanted*.** Minutes later he was arrested at a casino on an Indian reservation in Arizona. He went back to jail.

Eventually he got out. This time I did hear from him. He needed money, and he wanted me to send it via Western Union. But, he promised, he was owed a settlement from the prison for tens of thousands of dollars and would be able to pay me back soon. I was making next to nothing, and my wife was making less, but we gave him what we could. Soon, he called again. He needed more money. We gave him more. Not much later, the phone rang again. He needed more. We gave more. Finally, he asked again, and this time I told him

---

*Later my father would be featured in biographies about Ted Williams with a list of some of the aliases he used—Vince Addison, Nick Addison, William Addison, Vincent Villa, Vincent Hurst, John Shuffle—and an explanation that he had been "arrested thirty different times and convicted at least seven times on charges ranging from writing bad checks to second-degree grand theft; he was a certified con man."[1]

**My picture was also shown. Yeah.

we had no more to give. We didn't hear from him for a while after that. Finally, after several months, the phone rang. He told me his settlement had come in, and he wanted to know how much he had borrowed from us. I estimated that it was about $3,000. He said he was at Western Union and was sending the money he owed us at that very moment. It was a huge relief. I rushed down to Western Union, but . . . there was no money. I should have figured.

I drove home and called him but discovered that in the time it took me to get to Western Union and back (maybe twenty-five minutes?), he had moved. I guess he felt some need to make me believe he was paying me back, and after convincing me of that lie, he raced out of town. I should have figured.

That phone call promising me that money was the last I ever heard from my father.

A few years later the phone rang, but this time it was my uncle. He told me my father had died. He'd had a heart attack in a hotel room in New Orleans and wasn't found for several days. They thought I should know. They had decided there would be no need for a funeral.

I found it difficult to pretend I cared.

I hated him.

The only emotion I felt was relief. The nightmare he had put me and so many others through was finally over.

Scott's Downward Spiral

Scott and I sat in a coffee shop down the street from the casinos where he had ruined his life. He shared his story. . . .

Scott and his wife were going through a rough patch in 1994. His wife started taking their kids to church. Scott followed. In that church he fell in love with God and gave his life to Jesus. It became the most amazing time in his life.

In 2002, Scott moved his family to Santa Barbara for a new job with a real-estate investor. That's when things started going wrong. Perhaps the biggest problem was that Santa Barbara was too close to Las Vegas.

Scott had struggled with compulsive gambling for most of his life. It started with poker games in high school, then fraternity blackjack games in college. He got married and, living in Texas, didn't have many opportunities to gamble. But on each of his occasional work trips to Las Vegas, he would find himself at a blackjack table, losing all the money he had on him.

Something happened in Santa Barbara. He slowly lost his focus on God and increasingly found himself obsessing over money. He started trying to keep up with rich people who were way wealthier than he could ever realistically hope to be. And he began making trips to Vegas. Repeatedly. It was there that his gambling addiction, mostly dormant for more than a decade, erupted.

On his first trip, he lost $20,000 in one weekend. It was a lot of money, but he was making enough to cover up the loss.

The problem was that his gambling addiction kept spiraling.

Scott started borrowing money from everyone he knew. He needed cash for gambling. He was lying to his wife and kids. He would be at his son's soccer game but never look up from his phone because he was frantically checking the scores of games he had bet on. He missed birthday parties because he couldn't pull himself away from the casino to get back home. All he could think about was gambling. It had become the most important thing in his world.

Soon he owed several *million* dollars to casinos in Vegas.

He owed his bookie $200,000.

He hadn't paid back his family and friends, and he would never be able to.

The lies were catching up to him.

Everything was falling apart.

Some friends confronted him. They said they wanted to help. They had found a rehab center he could go to in Texas, and they would pay for his treatment. Scott said yes before they could finish their offer.

He couldn't believe what he had become. He wanted to change. He flew out to Texas, thinking that he had hit rock bottom and would now start to get his life back again.

And *that's* when he hit rock bottom.

Scott was a couple of days into rehab when he learned that his wife had filed for divorce. Bookies had shown up at Scott's home, making threats about what would happen if they didn't receive their money. Outlandish credit-card bills filled the mailbox. Casinos were calling, demanding payment on the markers Scott had taken out, and promising they would prosecute if not paid promptly.

In his last week before entering rehab, unable to make

a bet with his regular bookie, Scott had someone refer him to a person who would take his bet. Scott put six thousand down on a game and lost. It turned out Scott had placed a bet with the Mexican Mafia. While Scott was in rehab, they showed up at the house, tried to break in, and threatened to hurt Scott's wife and friends if they weren't paid. Scott's friends were so scared that they paid the money Scott owed.

One morning Scott was sitting at breakfast when the director of the rehab facility walked in. "I need to see you," he said. Scott's hopes sank. He followed the director into his office and was handed a letter. It was from the friends who were paying for his rehab. They explained that they had heard from Scott's wife, they had talked to Scott's pastor, and they just didn't have any more grace to offer. Scott had done too much. He had gone too far. They would not pay for the rehab. The letter gave Scott two options: he could go to a transition house in San Diego, or he could go and stay with his parents in Texas. The friends would pay for Scott's plane ticket. Then they were done with him.

Scott walked out of the office. He wasn't willing to take either of the options presented to him, so he had to come up with a plan. Then it hit him. He had one more asset—a country-club membership in Santa Barbara. He immediately got on the phone to try and sell it. He would take the money he'd make off the sale, go to Las Vegas, and either win enough to pay everyone back and make things right, or lose and blow his brains out.

While he was trying to sell his country-club membership,

his sister called. She had done research and found another rehab facility, one that specialized in gambling. They had a bed available for him. She and his parents would pay. Scott said no. His sister started screaming at him, "You have to go! You have to go!"

Scott went, and it changed everything.

He went through eight one-hour therapy sessions every day for six weeks. The therapy was painful—and revealing. Scott desperately wanted to be fixed. The counselors helped him unpack his childhood. He began to understand what drove him to gambling and why he had no impulse control. He was given tools to fight off his urges to gamble. And he was hit with the gravity of what he had done. As he sat alone on Thanksgiving, and then on Christmas, without even a phone call from his wife or kids or friends, he kept asking himself, *How did I get here?* And he decided that, with God's help, he would never go back to his old ways. When he walked out of rehab, he would start a new life.

Scott knew he had spent years ignoring God, but he counted on the fact that while he was faithless, God had remained faithful.[2] Scott knew his love for God had proved unreliable, but God's love for him was anything but. The Bible promised him that in Romans 8:35-39:

> Who shall separate us from the love of Christ? Shall trouble or hardship or persecution or famine or nakedness or danger or sword? As it is written:

"For your sake we face death all day long;
    we are considered as sheep to be slaughtered."

No, in all these things we are more than conquerors
through him who loved us. For I am convinced that
neither death nor life, neither angels nor demons,
neither the present nor the future, nor any powers,
neither height nor depth, nor anything else in all
creation, will be able to separate us from the love of
God that is in Christ Jesus our Lord.

A Fresh Start?

Scott walked out of rehab knowing he was not the same
person. But all everyone else could see was . . . the same
person. He thought his family and friends would give him
a fresh start, but the reception he received was exactly the
opposite.

He was no longer welcome at his church. Occasionally he
had to show up there to pick up his son. When he walked in
to get him, other parents would look away. Scott would show
up at the Christian school his son attended, and the teachers
and other parents would turn away.

The Bible told him that nothing could separate him from
the love of Christ, but what he had done *had* separated him
from the love of Christ's followers. Ironically, the verses that
immediately precede the promise that nothing can separate
us from God's love prohibit Christians from bringing charges
against or condemning others:

What, then, shall we say in response to these things?
If God is for us, who can be against us? He who
did not spare his own Son, but gave him up for us
all—how will he not also, along with him, graciously
give us all things? Who will bring any charge against
those whom God has chosen? It is God who justifies.
Who then is the one who condemns? No one.
Christ Jesus who died—more than that, who was
raised to life—is at the right hand of God and is also
interceding for us.[3]

Scott looked at me over his empty coffee cup. "I thought
these people would all reach out to me, help me, but they
didn't. I was a pariah. Everyone has grace for the guy who
wasn't a Christian, lived a sinful life, and then came to church
and repented. But what about the guy who *was* a Christian
and then fell off the cliff? I learned that the Christian community isn't all that warm and fuzzy. And I didn't want to
open myself up to being judged anymore. So I decided I
couldn't be around Christians. I couldn't ever go back to
church."

Scott paused. "And that's when I heard about you and I
sent you that e-mail."

I thought back to receiving Scott's e-mail. It had said
something like, "I feel like I need to get in touch with you. I
am a compulsive gambler. I've ruined almost every relationship in my life, and I need a friend. Can I come to Las Vegas
and meet with you?"

The air was thick, not only with the smell of coffee, but also with a sense of irony. Scott was looking for someone who wouldn't hold his gambling addiction against him and who would extend God's grace to him—and he came to a pastor whose life had been destroyed by a gambling addict. I half expected someone to pop out with a hidden camera and tell me I was being punked.

How was I supposed to feel about Scott?

And how did God feel about him? If there was one kind of person it was difficult for me to think God could be for, this was it.

Can God forgive serial killers? Of course he can.

Can God forgive Adolf Hitler? Yes, I believe he can.

But can God forgive conniving gambling addicts who destroy the lives of their little sons? Why would he?

Looking at Scott, hearing his story, I realized Scott was the *last* kind of person I would want to extend grace to, the most difficult for me to forgive.

And in that moment it hit me: that's what the Bible said God did for *me*. I wasn't someone it was easy for God to extend grace to, easy for God to forgive. I had done too much. I had gone too far. But it was right then, when I was at my most sinful, when I had made God my enemy, that God demonstrated his love for me. When I was at my absolute worst, God allowed the absolute worst possible thing to happen—Jesus died for me.[4]

How could I receive that from God and not give it to Scott?

To take it further: How could I receive that from God and not give it to my father?

I suffered so much because of a gambling addict; it's not easy for me to think that God could be for them. But he is.

Maybe that's part of the beauty of grace. God is for the person you least expect or want him to be for.

And it's pretty cool, because I'm probably last on someone's list of people they want God to be for.

And it's pretty cool, because you probably are too.

5

GOD FOR
DYSFUNCTIONAL FAMILIES

DONNIE FOUND HIMSELF in a motel with two guys and a lady.
He watched the three of them take turns on a crack pipe, and
then the two men take turns on the lady. What was happening was probably not that unusual for a seedy motel room
in the Watts neighborhood of Los Angeles. Except the lady
was Donnie's mother. And Donnie was only five years old.

My Hotel Room
I had a life-defining motel room experience of my own. It
wasn't with my mother and some random guys. Actually, it
wasn't with anyone.

I was seven years old. My father had just led us on another

get-out-of-town-in-the-middle-of-the-night adventure. My mother and sister drove our car and stopped along the way. My dad and I drove straight through from our never-to-be-seen-again home in New Jersey to a who-knows-where-we're-going destination in Florida in a rented truck. The two of us had dinner at a restaurant, where my father kept talking to the waitress. Soon we were paying at the cash register.

There was a motel just across the parking lot, and we drove over and got a room. That's when my father told me I'd be staying by myself. I didn't understand. He said he had something he had to do. Honestly, I'm not sure whether I understood it was the waitress. I insisted that I was too young and too afraid to stay by myself. He told me he would lock the door and I would be fine. Then he left.

I don't know what was the most painful: being alone and afraid, or knowing my father would belittle me for being afraid when he came back, or the thought that he might not come back at all. Part of me hoped he wouldn't. I would have loved to never see him again. But no one knew where I was. What would happen to me?

I decided I wasn't going to wait to find out. I didn't want to live like this anymore. There was an ashtray on the dresser. I took it into the bathroom and threw it into the bathtub. It broke into hundreds of pieces. I picked up one of the bigger shards of glass with the intention of slitting my wrists, but I couldn't fully commit. I hated my life enough to want to die, and now I hated myself for not being strong enough to make it happen. I felt pathetic.

I worked long into the night picking up every tiny little sliver of glass and flushing each one down the toilet so my father wouldn't know what I'd done. When he showed up in the morning, I acted like being alone was no big deal, and we continued on our totally fun adventure.[1]

That story does not completely epitomize my childhood. It was more of a lowlight. But looking back on my growing-up years, I realize I had a dysfunctional family. My wife would say that's an understatement.

And coming from a dysfunctional family has scarred me in all kinds of ways.

It's led me to a low sense of self-worth.

I've questioned whether I'm capable of being loved.

I've wondered if perhaps my background disqualifies me from doing ministry, or at least makes me unable to have a significant impact with my life. Maybe I'm just too messed up to make a difference.

I've felt like I could never recover enough to be a good husband and father.

Now before I come on too strong with this victim card, let me tell you that I do realize others have had it worse.

Like Donnie . . .

Donnie

Donnie was born in Compton. Compton is infamous as a stronghold of the Los Angeles gangs the Bloods, the Crips, and the Sureños.

He was born to two drug addicts. His dad disappeared

early on, leaving his mother to raise him. Donnie was shuttled back and forth between his grandmother in Compton and his mother, who was living in Watts—the only part of L.A. that's possibly worse than Compton.

Most nights Donnie slept on the floor in the corner of a crack house. His mother would usually be smoking crack or sleeping somewhere in the same room. Occasionally she would wake him up in the middle of the night. They would go out into the darkness, scanning the gang-ridden streets for aluminum cans. When they finally collected enough, Donnie's mom would turn the cans in for money, so she could go back and buy more drugs at the crack house.

God Was for Me. So What?

So, yes, I understand others had it worse than I did.

And I feel worse for Donnie than I do for me, but . . . I still feel bad for me.

Now I know God is for me. He was for me even back when I was going through my Three Mile Island childhood. But when you've gone through or are going through that kind of pain, there's something lacking when someone tells you they're "for you."

I can be for my friend battling cancer, but that feels somewhat hollow. I'm not the one going through chemo. I don't have to face the thought of my daughter having no dad to walk her down the aisle at her wedding. My friend does.

If you haven't walked in someone's shoes, just being "for them" somehow seems inadequate.

But that's *exactly* what Jesus did. He walked in our shoes. He walked in *my* shoes.

My parents weren't married when I was conceived. Neither were Jesus'. And he had it even worse than I did, because growing up in a close-knit and extremely religious town, everyone would have known and would have looked down on him as "the bastard kid."

Like I told you before, my father thought he was wanted by the FBI.* We went into hiding and lived life on the run. At Jesus' birth a paranoid king wanted him dead, so Jesus' family had to go into hiding and live life on the run.

My father would continually go on long trips or just disappear. Finally, when I was eleven, he left and never came back. I had to grow up without a father. It seems that Jesus' dad died young, so Jesus was without a father. But Jesus had it even worse—I rode shotgun in a U-Haul truck, whereas Jesus was probably on the back of a donkey.

I didn't grow up in a home that was as supportive as it should have been. One time when Jesus was teaching, his mother and brothers showed up and told everyone he had lost his mind and they wanted to take him home.[2] It's unbelievable. Can you picture what Jesus must have been thinking? *Are you serious? Mom? Mary! Are you kidding? An angel*

---

*He registered under a fake name, and my birth certificate announced that "Vincent Shuffle" had come into the world. My father, whose name was Vincent Antonucci, then had a fake birth certificate made for me with the name "Vincent Antonucci," and that's the one we used. (Don't ask me why he gave me a real birth certificate with a fake name and a fake birth certificate with what should have been my real name. Like I said, he was paranoid.) Anyway, I grew up thinking my name was Vincent Antonucci. It wasn't until I was fifteen that I found out my real name was Vincent Shuffle, at which point I had my name legally changed to Vincent Antonucci.

showed up. You got pregnant by a ghost! Shepherds showed up at my birth. Wise men brought baby shower gifts. And you don't get this? You're *not behind me?*

Jesus had a dysfunctional family. The things I went through, he went through. The Bible says he was "a man of sorrows and acquainted with grief."[3]

And because of that, God being for us is not just some theoretical platitude for old Christian ladies to cross-stitch and put up on their living room walls. It is real and powerful and life changing. Jesus shared in our flesh-and-blood existence, he went through the same struggles we do, and he understands how we feel. So we can go to him with confidence, and we can find real help in our time of need.[4]

Donnie's Reversal

At this point in the story, Donnie was almost seven years old. He didn't know his last name. He couldn't spell his first name. He couldn't even spell c-a-t. His mother had never thought to put him in school. He couldn't count to three.

One day he was sitting on a curb outside the crack house when a car drove past, stopped, then backed up in front of him. The lady driving the car looked out the passenger side window. "Are you Donnie?"

Donnie didn't recognize this person but said yes.

She said, "I'm your sister."

Donnie felt embarrassed and pretended to know who she was.

She looked concerned. "Donnie, get in the car."

Donnie followed orders.

"Donnie, is our mother inside?"

Donnie nodded yes.

"I'll be right back." Donnie's sister went into the house, found their mother, and told her that she wanted to have Donnie over to spend the night. Her mother was too high to care.

Donnie's sister brought him to her home. She told him, "Donnie, I'm not taking you back there. You need to be in a better environment." Donnie didn't know what to think, but agreed.

She asked, "Do you know your birthday?"

This was one thing Donnie *did* know. He smiled and told her with pride, "July 30." His birthday wasn't coming soon, but his sister smiled and said, "I'm going to throw you a birthday party!"

Party day arrived, and even Donnie's father, whom Donnie had rarely seen, showed up. Donnie was in the yard, playing in a big, empty box. His father yelled at him to get out of it. Donnie couldn't pull himself away. His dad yelled again. Donnie was so absorbed that he continued playing in the box. His father came over and punched him in the face. Donnie had never been hit. In shock he ran into the house and upstairs to his sister. His sister asked what had happened, and after Donnie explained, she exploded down the stairs. Donnie followed. She started pushing their father and demanding that he leave. Donnie recalls, "That was the first time I ever felt safe. There was someone willing to fight for me."

Donnie's sister put him in school. He started in second grade. Because he was way behind, he had to repeat second grade, but his sister made him work hard, and soon he started getting straight As. At thirteen, Donnie moved with his sister to Las Vegas. He graduated from high school and went to college. Donnie married his high school sweetheart, and they started a family of their own.

One day something strange happened. Donnie's sister-in-law started going to church. And not just going—she loved it. Neither family had any churchgoers or any faith, but now they were all hearing rave reviews about this church where the messages made sense, you could wear what you wanted, and they even provided day care for your kids. Donnie kept telling her, "Religion isn't for me," but finally decided to try it.

I'll never forget baptizing Donnie. The smile on his face may have been the biggest one I've ever seen. I wonder if maybe it was because Donnie finally had a father and a new family who loved him and made home a safe place.

When Donnie's wife had their fourth child, she had some complications that forced her to stay in the hospital. My wife and I went to visit her. We cared, and that's what pastors do. Most people appreciate such a visit, but Donnie seemed genuinely shocked by it. Coming from a dysfunctional background, I get that.

Today, Donnie is one of my favorite people, and he's one of the most attentive fathers I know.

Redeemed

I always wondered if I could find someone to love me. I mean, even my own father, who was obligated to love me, didn't. I always doubted that I could be a good dad. What did I know about being even an adequate father? And I doubted I could be an effective pastor; I just didn't have the pedigree for it.

Today, the best things I have going for me are my wife and kids. For some reason, they love me, and I think I keep getting better at loving them.

Today, the best thing I have going for me as a pastor is that our church reaches lots of "messy" people who relate to my messy background.

God has redeemed my dysfunctional past and translated it into the most functional parts of my life today.

You

Perhaps you have some dysfunction in your family.

Remember:

Jesus' great-great-great-great-great- (times a couple more) grandmother was a prostitute.

Jesus' great-great-great-great (times a couple more) grandfather was an adulterer who killed his mistress's husband to cover up the infidelity.

Jesus' mother was an unmarried teenager.

Jesus grew up poor, from a little backwoods, redneck town that people made fun of.

His family thought he was crazy.

That's how God *chose* to come into the world. He could have had an easy life, but he *chose* to live in dysfunction.

Why?

Because he is for you. And he *wanted* to go through what you've *had* to go through. So he could understand how you feel, and so he could help you grow past it.

You can turn to him as an empathetic and trusted friend. And not only does he understand, but he has the power to get you through what you have to get through, so you can go where you need to go.

6

GOD FOR THE DOUBTERS

I LOVE IT when people respond in ways I'd never expect. My favorite surprising responses seem to come from my wife. Like on our first anniversary when we went to a fancy restaurant.* We ordered, our food came to the table, and Jen tasted it and exclaimed, "Ugh! That tastes like body odor!" Body odor? *Not* what I expected.

Just recently someone paid for us to go to another fancy restaurant. We ordered a salad. Jen took a bite and sputtered, "No! That tastes like a Navy ship!"

"What are you talking about?" I asked. "When have you ever tasted a Navy ship?"

---

*Well, it may not have been that fancy, but when you're used to McDonald's . . .

She asked me, "Have you ever been on a Navy ship?"

"Yes."

"Then you know," she said, "that if you tasted a Navy ship, this salad is exactly what it would taste like!"

Not the reaction I expected.

The first surprising response I ever got from my wife was . . . the *first* response I ever got from my wife, long before she became my wife. During my undergraduate years of college I worked at a movie theater. I'm pretty silly. I do goofy things. At the theater, people would wait in line to buy their tickets in a little, glass-enclosed foyer that had great acoustics. So when no one was in line to buy tickets, I would go to the foyer and sing in it. I would do my best opera impersonations or sing "Immigrant Song" by Led Zeppelin. And whoever was selling tickets at the time would just stare at me like "You are an idiot." But there was one ticket-seller girl, Jennifer, who would smile and laugh. And I thought, "Wow, no one else responds that way to my extraordinary singing ability!"

At that time I was a new Christian, and I was trying to talk to everyone about Jesus. I felt like everyone needed to know that God is for us, and Jesus came for us. So I decided to talk to this Jen with the amazing ear for superb musical talent. But because she worked in the ticket window, facing out toward the street, and I worked *inside* the theater, we never had a good opportunity to talk. So I decided to write her a note. One day during my break I wrote a note explaining that I had just become a Christian because it turns out the Bible is true, and Jesus is real, and God loves us.

I was sharing that with a lot of people at the time, and some of the responses I was getting were negative. Jen had gone to church a little when she was growing up but had already discarded her faith, if she'd ever really had any. My expectations were low. But Jen responded in a surprising way. She told me she wanted to see if there was truth in Christianity. She didn't believe, but she was open to the possibility of faith. So we started getting together, and she asked all kinds of questions. And I began to show her the evidence for Jesus—that he really lived, actually died for our sins, and truly rose from the dead. The evidence convinced Jen that Jesus is real. And reading about Jesus convinced her that Jesus is really for her. She fell in love with him and decided to give her life to him.

Well, soon I was the one asking questions. Questions like:

Wait, do I like this Jen girl? I do.

Does she like me? I think she does.

Do I like, like *this Jen?* I think I do!

But does she like, like *me?* I think she does!

Wait, do I love this Jen? Uh-oh. I think I do.

What if she doesn't love me? Wait, is it possible she loves me? I think she loves me!

And then, *Could she be* the *one?* Maybe not. But what if? Wait, she is!

Should I ask her to marry me? When should I ask her? What if she says no? But what if she says yes?

And eventually, I did ask her, and she did say yes, and about twenty years ago we got married.

God's Response to Doubt

Maybe you have something in common with my wife. Perhaps you're someone who has discarded your faith, if you ever really had any. Maybe when I mention evidence for the Bible and for Jesus, you're skeptical. Or perhaps you do believe but also have some doubts.

And perhaps you think that because you have doubts, God's reaction to you would be negative.

You assume that God's attitude would be, "If you're going to discard your faith in me, I'm going to discard my faith in *you*. If you're done with me, I'm done with you. If you have doubts about me, I have doubts about you."

If you think that, you're going to be surprised at God's reaction to doubters. Let me share some more stories with surprising responses, because I love surprising responses.

You may have doubts about the Bible's claim that God came to earth in the person of Jesus, that Jesus exactly represents God and *is* God. At the time of Jesus, people weren't sure about that either. Some believed; others didn't.

The first person to believe was John.* John was a cousin of Jesus and most likely grew up hearing about his cousin's miraculous birth. John was given the role of introducing Jesus to the world. He baptized Jesus. He saw a dove come down from heaven to celebrate Jesus' baptism. He heard a voice boom out from heaven, "This is my Son, in whom I am well pleased."[1] He witnessed Jesus' miracles.

---

*The John we call John the Baptist. (Not the apostle John . . . or John Wayne . . . or John Mayer . . . or any other John.)

But then, a few years later, John started to have doubts. He wasn't sure anymore.

By the way, the reason John began to doubt was because he'd been put in prison for speaking against immorality. He felt like, *I'm living for God. I'm in prison for it, and God's not doing anything about it. So maybe this whole thing isn't true.*

Maybe your doubts have been driven by circumstances. You feel like there's no way a good God would allow this bad thing to happen in your life, so there must not be a good God.

Or perhaps your doubts are more intellectual. You had a science teacher tell you there's no God. No one has ever answered your questions. So you're skeptical that God exists.

It could be that your doubts are more relationally driven. You may have met some hypocritical Christians and decided, "If that's what Christians are like, I'm not interested."

Or maybe you had an absent or abusive father. Nearly all the famous atheists of our time had absent or abusive fathers. I don't think that's a coincidence. I know from my own experience that it's easy to come to the conclusion, "If that's what fathers are like, then I want nothing to do with this idea of a heavenly Father."

Our doubts can be driven by many causal factors. For John, it was his circumstances. He found himself in prison, and Jesus didn't come to his rescue.

So John sent some messengers to his cousin to ask, "Are you really the one? Are you really God come for us?"

What would you guess happened here? I might assume Jesus would say, "What kind of question is that? God gave you this special role, and you're questioning it? How dare you? You baptized me. You saw the dove. You heard the voice. You know about the miracles. And now you doubt? That's it!"

I would be wrong.

Because when Jesus heard John's question and doubts, his surprising response was to send the messengers back to reassure John that yes, he *was* the one, he was still doing miracles, he was still proving that he was God. And then Jesus turned to the crowd who was watching this and he said, "I tell you, among those born of women there is no one greater than John."[2]

John, who should have been more sure than anyone else, expressed serious doubts, and Jesus gave him the ultimate compliment. It turns out that God is for the doubter.

Here's another story.

Jesus had been doing all kinds of miracles. He'd even raised people from the dead. Thousands had witnessed his power, and everyone was talking about it.

There was a man who had a sick son, so he brought his son to Jesus. He stood in front of Jesus, looked at him, and said, "*If* you can do anything, take pity on us and help us."[3]

What would you guess would happen here? I might assume Jesus would have said, "'*If* you can?' If? Have you not been paying attention? Do you have so little faith? Well, then, no I can't, because you don't have enough faith for me to do this miracle for you."

I would be wrong again.

Here's what actually happened next: "'If you can'?" said Jesus. "Everything is possible for one who believes."[4]

Jesus kind of came back with an "if" of his own. It's like he was saying, "The 'if' isn't about me. It's about *you*. Because if you believe, anything and everything is possible."

So how did the father respond?

If I were him, I would have said, "Of course I believe! Did I say 'if'? I meant 'Since.' I meant, '*Since* you can do anything, take pity on us and help us.'"

But that's not what he said. Here's his surprising response: "Immediately the boy's father exclaimed, 'I do believe; help me overcome my unbelief!'"[5]

He was basically saying, "I do believe! But I also *don't* believe! I have faith, but I have doubts. Help me!"

So how would Jesus react to that? Maybe with, "I'm appalled. I expect total faith. I gave you two chances!" and then stomping off in disgust?

No, Jesus' surprising response was to speak to the man's son and to heal him, just as the doubting father requested. It turns out that God is for the doubter.

I'll give you one more story.

Jesus recruited some guys to be his twelve disciples, his apprentices. They became best friends. Jesus trained them. And he taught them, repeatedly, that he would die and then three days later rise from the dead.

Eventually Jesus was arrested, tortured, and killed. And three days later one of Jesus' best friends, one of his apprentices, was alone when suddenly the rest of the group showed up and excitedly told him that it had actually happened! Jesus *had* risen! They had seen him!

And this guy's attitude was, "Yeah, right. You expect me to believe that?" In fact, he said, "Unless I see the nail marks in his hands and put my finger where the nails were, and put my hand into his side, I will not believe."[6] Thomas was saying to his friends, "I don't believe you. You're lying to me. And Jesus lied to us when he said he would come back from death."

So what would you guess happened here? I might assume Jesus would have gone to Thomas and said, "You're no longer one of my apprentices. You're fired, no longer one of my friends. In fact, let me delete you from the contacts on my phone."

I would be wrong.

Because instead of firing Thomas, Jesus' surprising response was to show up a few days later, walk right up to Thomas, and say, "'Put your finger here; see my hands. Reach out your hand and put it into my side. Stop doubting and believe.' Thomas said to him, 'My Lord and my God!'"[7] Jesus addressed Thomas's doubts and led Thomas to faith.

How cool is all that?

Think about it: How would you handle it if a friend of yours, or your spouse, expressed such a lack of faith in you, such doubt about you? What if they fired questions at you about your character? Or if before you went on your business trip, your wife said, "*If* you can be faithful while you're gone, it would be nice." Or if you made a promise, and someone told your friend that you kept your promise, and your friend said, "Yeah, right. You expect me to believe that?"

You probably wouldn't handle it very well, would you? I wouldn't! We'd be angry. But God is a God of grace. And God can handle your questions. He understands your doubt. He believes in you even if you're not sure you believe in him. And he is *for* doubters.

Doubt: Curse or Gift?

I hope you're encouraged to know that if you're just naturally skeptical, or if things you've gone through have caused you to doubt, that doesn't affect how God feels about you. God is still for you.

But you may still have a question: Why? It's nice that God isn't against us because of our doubts, but why does God allow us to have doubts? Why doesn't God make himself more obvious, so believing in him is easy?

It's because he loves you.

I believe your uncertainty is a *gift* from God.

We think we want certainty, for God to make himself obvious so we can't doubt his existence. But maybe God's goal isn't for us to just acknowledge that he exists.

I'll never forget the day my son looked at me and said without prompting, "Daddy, I love you." He had said it back to me before, but this time it was all on his own. Wow. That is one of the best things a parent can hear! But what if, instead, he looked up at me and said, "Daddy, I acknowledge you exist." That . . . would not be so hot.

God could make himself obvious, and we would have to believe in him. But that wouldn't mean we'd *love* him. And God's goal is love.

Uncertainty may not extinguish doubt, but it actually *does* help fan the flames of love. John Ortberg puts it this way:

> André Comte-Sponville notes that it is precisely the experience of uncertainty that makes possible the euphoria of what we call falling in love. We go through intense questioning, wondering, hoping, and doubting. *Does she really care?* And when that is followed by evidence that she *does* care, we have an endorphin tidal wave. It is precisely this roller-coaster ride of the agony of uncertainty and the ecstasy of relief that gives the early stages of love their emotional TNT.[8]

So maybe uncertainty is a gift because it gives us the possibility of that kind of relationship with God. And maybe what we really want isn't certainty but a love relationship.

I wrote earlier about when I first met my wife and how the uncertainty led to an emotional roller coaster that ultimately led to love. Here's some of the story of when I first met God.

I am one of the most skeptical people you could ever meet. I assume everything's a lie and everyone's out to get me. I was raised in an atheistic home, never taken to church, and never heard God mentioned. My mother is an atheist to this day. So I grew up with 100 percent doubt, 0 percent faith.

On Easter morning of my sophomore year of college, I

saw a preacher on TV for a just minute, and he was talking about evidence for the Bible. I sneered at that. I was a pre-law major. I was into evidence, knew all about evidence, and the idea that there would be evidence for something in the Bible made me laugh. I thought it was akin to saying, "Let me tell you about the evidence for the Little Mermaid."

But this preacher piqued my curiosity, so I borrowed a Bible. It was the first time I had ever touched one. I opened it, wondering how easy it would be to expose it as a myth and whether anyone had tried to do that. And if not, could I get my picture on the cover of *Time* magazine as the guy who brought down Christianity?

I expected the Bible to read like a fairy tale: "Once upon a time, there lived a man named Jesus, who did nice things for people, and performed miracles, and had a blue ox named Babe, and could lasso a tornado!" I was shocked when the Bible repeatedly gave times and places. One of the first chapters I read was Luke 3, which begins,

> In the fifteenth year of the reign of Tiberius Caesar—
> when Pontius Pilate was governor of Judea, Herod
> tetrarch of Galilee, his brother Philip tetrarch of Iturea
> and Traconitis, and Lysanias tetrarch of Abilene—
> during the high-priesthood of Annas and Caiaphas,
> the word of God came to John son of Zechariah in
> the wilderness. He went into all the country around
> the Jordan, preaching a baptism of repentance for the
> forgiveness of sins.[9]

My response was . . . surprise. That was a lot of detail for a myth! And if you give a time and place, there *could* be evidence to prove the event did or didn't happen.

So my curiosity grew, and I kept reading. I kept reading for months. Hours a day, every day, for months. I read the Bible and tried to find evidence that would invalidate it. But all the evidence actually pointed to the validity of the Bible. My curiosity was turning into confusion.

As I continued to read, the craziest thing happened. I was drawn to the central character, Jesus. He was amazing. I thought, *If this guy was real, he had to be God, because no one else could live like this. He was perfect, but he didn't demand perfection from others. He taught a way of life no one else had taught, and he actually lived it. He was funny, inspiring, and compassionate.*

I realized that Jesus was so amazing that, if he was real, I would want to be around him all the time.

Then, as I continued to read about him, something dawned on me: *I think Jesus would choose to be around me.* I knew I was a total screwup. So if there was a God, I would never imagine he'd be interested in me. But this Jesus I was reading about, who was God in the flesh, hung out with really screwed-up people. He liked them.

I wondered, *Is it possible he could like me?* Then, *Well, it doesn't matter, because he's not real.*

But then I examined more evidence and thought, *I believe he is real. Could all this be true? What if it is true?*

And I read that God was offering a relationship to people.

I asked, *Could I have a relationship with God? Would he want to have a relationship with me? What would that look like? What would it do to my life?*

I read more and realized, *I think he does, and I think I can actually have this.*

Then I wondered, *Should I say yes to this? Do I really believe this? Oh my goodness, I do. I believe this. I think I want to say yes. God loves me. And . . . I love God. I want God. I want to have a relationship with God forever.*

It was an endorphin tidal wave like I had never experienced before, and never will again. I loved God!

And *that's* what God is after.

If God made himself obvious—as if he were this undeniable giant that hovered in the sky above us—I would have acknowledged his existence my entire life. I would have always believed in his existence. But would I have loved him? I don't know.

Would I have had that emotional roller-coaster experience that threw me into the relationship I still have with him today? I don't think so, because it's the experience of uncertainty that makes possible the euphoria of falling in love.

I think that uncertainty is a gift.

Choosing to Live by Faith?

Even when we've come to a place of greater certainty, like I'm in today, having *some* uncertainty, some doubts along the way, is a good thing. A guy named Frederick Buechner writes, "Doubts are the ants in the pants of faith. They keep it awake and moving." A little uncertainty can lead us to pursue more truth and find the answers we need, so our faith can grow and our beliefs can become even more grounded.

The cool thing is that there *is* truth and there *are* answers. When I began to do research, I quickly discovered that *many* people had tried to disprove the Christian faith. Intelligent people like Pulitzer Prize–winning journalists and Harvard law professors. And I read story after story, book after book, by those who had sought to tear down the Christian faith only to come to faith and turn to Christ. As I began to reach the conclusion that the Bible was true (and even today when doubts creep in), it has helped me to know that very smart people have faith.

But honestly, my skeptical nature still fought against the idea of "putting my faith" in something and choosing to "live by faith." I believed the Bible was true, and I wanted Jesus, but the faith part still bothered me. I didn't think of myself as a "faith" kind of person.

Then one day, pretty early in my journey, I realized I was wrong. I wasn't switching to faith; I had always lived by faith. I wasn't choosing faith; all of us have no choice but to live by faith.

I'll explain by telling you about my first sermon. It wasn't really a sermon, but as someone who now preaches sermons just about every week, I kind of look back on it as my first sermon.

After becoming a Christian, I started attending a campus ministry. One day every year this group would set up a stage in a courtyard where kids ate lunch. Throughout the day, they would have some of the students from the ministry share their faith with anyone who would listen. They asked me to speak for a few minutes. I was freaked out. I was a new Christian and had never done anything like that. But I said yes, and I started working on what I'd say. When I finally had it written, I read it over enough so I could (very nervously) present it without notes.

I later learned that what I came up with was originally thought up and presented in the 1600s by a mathematician and philosopher named Blaise Pascal. It's been called Pascal's Wager, but I had never heard of it. I thought I made it up.* Here are the basics of what I said that day in the courtyard:

> Whether or not you've ever realized it, you are making a bet with your life. We are all making a bet with our lives.
>
> You're either betting that God is real and Jesus was his Son, the Savior, or you're betting that he's not. There is no third option.
>
> If you bet that God is real and you're *right*, then you live a life devoted to love and compassion and generosity, and when you die, you go to heaven to forever be with the God who loves you.
>
> If you make that bet and you're *wrong*, then you

---

*I used a six-pack of cereal boxes as an illustration at the beginning of my talk—something I'm quite sure Blaise Pascal did not include in his argument. Apparently, compared to me, he was a theological lightweight.

live a life of love and compassion and generosity, and when you die you will rot in a grave because it turns out there is no God.

But if, instead, you make the bet that God is *not* real and you're right, then when you die you will rot in a grave, right next to the Christians who were wrong.

If you make that bet and you're *wrong*, then you lose everything. You lose out on the meaning and purpose of your life, and you lose the chance to be with a loving God for all eternity in heaven.

So if you bet on God and Jesus, ultimately there's really *nothing* to lose; there's only *everything* to gain.

But if you bet *against* God, ultimately there's really *nothing* to gain; there's only *everything* to *lose*.

And here's the thing—the gamble you're making isn't on whether you'll live by faith or not, because *everyone* lives by faith. You either have faith that God exists, or you have faith that he doesn't. But either way, it's faith.

I realize there may be some arguments *against* the existence of God that people who *don't* believe base their faith on.

But one thing you may not realize is that there are *definitely* arguments and all kinds of evidence *for* the existence of God, for the deity of Jesus, and for the validity of the Bible, that people who *do* believe base their faith on.

So don't think it's about whether you choose to live by faith. You *are* living by faith. Don't think that some people choose to make a gamble, placing their bet that there is a God. We *all* have to make a wager.

The difference isn't faith, or whether you'll take a gamble with your life. It's just, who are you going to bet on? Will you wager there is a God or there's not?

Just to be clear, you shouldn't place your faith in Jesus because he's a safer bet; that's not a reason to believe. But it is a reason to want to believe. It is a reason to be open to seeing if there's any truth in it. It is a reason to be open to the possibility of faith in Jesus.

I hope you start this journey of pursuing and discovering truth. And if you do, you'll find what I found. The evidence is much stronger that there is a God and that Jesus is his Son, who came for you in love.

That was my first little sermon about twenty-five years ago, and I would tell you the same thing today.

Except I now understand something else. I now realize that God made a wager too. He bet on *you* when he sent his Son, when he allowed his Son to sacrifice his life on a cross, so that if you believe, you can be saved. And he did it because he is for you, he loves you, and he wants to have a relationship with you.

7

GOD FOR THE TATTOOED

JOHNNY PAUSED THE DVD. Since there were no clients in the store, Johnny and Tommy were in the back, continuing their Harry Potter marathon.

Johnny said, "Hey—so, I guess I have a question about the Bible."

Tommy smiled. Finally. This was the first time Johnny had initiated a spiritual conversation.

"So, I've never read the Bible, but I know Jesus is in there," Johnny started, "and I've heard about the . . . what, the Virgin Mary? So, is there, like, a connection? Like between Mary and Jesus?"

"Are you being serious?" Tommy wasn't sure.

"Yeah," Johnny affirmed. "Are they connected?"

"Yeah," Tommy answered. "Actually, Mary was Jesus' mother."

"Oh, got it." Johnny seemed lost in thought. "One more question. The other person I've heard of in the Bible is Mother Teresa. So is she connected? How does she fit in the Bible with Mary and Jesus?"

Tommy was confused again. "Wait—are you serious or not?"

The look on Johnny's face let Tommy know he was. It was a sincere question.

Tommy told him, "No, man. Mother Teresa's not in the Bible. She just died not too long ago. She's from, like, our time."

Now Johnny was confused. "Wait," he questioned, "you guys aren't still writing the Bible?"

"No, it stopped being written almost two thousand years ago."

"Ohhh." This was obviously a major revelation to Johnny. "I had no idea."

Leaving Law School

I had become a Christian, and I was angry. I couldn't believe no one had ever mentioned Jesus to me, told me God loves me, or invited me to church. I now knew that Jesus' last and most imperative command was to make sure everyone knew the good news of God's love and had an opportunity to respond to it. Since no one had told me, I assumed Christians had decided to ignore what Jesus commanded. I refused to do the same. I wanted to make the biggest difference I could for God and help everyone to experience what I had finally experienced.

I had been planning on going to law school, so I did. And I loved law school but felt like I was in the wrong place, preparing for the wrong thing. This was not the path by which I would have the greatest impact for God's love revolution.

At the end of my first year, I was home for the summer and driving with my girlfriend. (The one who found my singing Led Zeppelin songs in the movie theater alcove irresistible. The one I'd later marry, who believes she knows what body odor and Navy ships taste like.) I took a deep breath. I told her I didn't think I was supposed to be in law school or become a lawyer. She nodded. "I think you're right."

"So what do I do?" I asked in my angsty voice. I had been planning on becoming a lawyer since about second grade.*

"I think you know," she said encouragingly. "You've known since the day you came to faith."

"Yeah, well, maybe." I was nervous. "But I have a full-ride scholarship to law school. I'll have no loans to repay. And the average first-year lawyer's salary is $80,000.** I looked at

*Some kids brought Incredible Hulk lunch boxes to school and talked about their Matchbox cars; I brought a briefcase and kept threatening to sue my classmates.
**And this was 1993, when a gallon of milk cost $2, versus today's price of almost $4. And gas was $1 a gallon, versus today's price of $3 or more. And the cost of an espresso macchiato at Starbucks was . . . well, unless you lived in the big city, there were no Starbucks, and the closest thing to a macchiato was an actor named Ralph from the Karate Kid movies.

seminary. I won't be able to get any scholarships. I'll have to pay about $15,000 a year. I'll have major school loans to repay. And first-year pastors get paid about $25,000."

Jen then made an incredible argument.

"So?"

That's what she said. She said, "So?"

Even with a year of law school under my belt, including a win in moot court, I couldn't refute her logic.

I met with the seminary admissions officer, who reminded me a little of Cliff Clavin from *Cheers*. He asked why I was thinking about transferring from law school. I told him, "I'm not coming here to learn the Bible. I can do that on my own. I don't need to pay you to do that. And I'm not coming here to learn how to pray, or . . . I don't know, whatever else you guys teach here. I can do that on my own."

"So," said the Cliff Clavin–impersonating admissions officer, looking puzzled, "why are you here?"

I looked him right in the eye. (You know, for effect, the power stare.) "I want to know how I can use my life to help the most people know Jesus. Can I major in that? Do you have that major?"

Cliff Clavin smiled. "Well, we *don't* have a major called 'How I Can Use My Life to Help the Most People Know Jesus,' but we *do* have one called 'Church Growth.' I think that's what you'd want."

I didn't have the debating skills to defeat Jen's "So?" but I was more prepared this time. I countered, "I'm not sure I totally understand what you mean by a church-growth major.

I want people to know Jesus and experience God's love like I have. Can you help me to do that or not?"

I couldn't tell if the admissions officer was getting annoyed, because he kept smiling. "Yes," he told me. "I think we can."

"Then I'm in. How long will it take me to graduate?"

Cliffy explained it was a two-year program. Then he said, laughing, "We had a guy once who did it in one year!"

"That sounds good," I told him. "I'll do it in one year."

"No, no," he sputtered. "I wasn't giving you an option. It's a two-year program. I was just remembering this crazy guy who took a double class load for two semesters and did the whole thing in one year. It was almost suicidal. You don't want to do that."

"Yes, I do." (He didn't know I'd won my moot court case. He wasn't going to win this debate by throwing around words like *crazy* and *suicidal*.)

"I would advise against that." He frowned. "Why would you want to do that?"

"Because," I answered, "I don't want to be here with a bunch of Christians learning how to help people know Jesus. I want to be out with a bunch of non-Christians, helping them to know Jesus." (I called that my "duh" defense.) "I just need to know the most effective way to do that. I can learn that in a year."

I did seminary in one year.

I discovered that the most effective way to help people who are uninterested in God to come to church is by starting a new one. That people who don't like church are more open to checking one out if it's new.

I signed up.

After my year at seminary, I did a couple of years as an intern and served as an associate pastor to get experience and to prepare. And then my wife and I moved to Virginia Beach, Virginia, to start a brand-new church.

Tommy

I met Tommy at that church.[1]

Tommy had recently gotten out of the Air Force. He was in a unit called the Air Force Special Operations.[*] Tommy dropped in behind enemy lines to prepare bomb sites in wars and knew how to kill people with his pinky or a rubber spatula. But those were his Chuck Norris days. Tommy was now in seminary. Like me, he had decided to become a pastor so he could make the biggest difference possible for God. When Tommy started attending our church, he began by volunteering and joining my small group.[**]

About two years later, during my twelfth year at that church, my wife and I felt God leading us to move to Las Vegas to start another church. After announcing it to everyone on a Sunday morning, we got together with our small group. As we shared our feelings with our group, Tommy had a big smile on his face. I wanted to tell him he was a jerk for being so happy we were leaving, but I

---

[*] I originally wrote, "in a unit called the Power Rangers," but I checked with Tommy because that didn't sound quite right. Turns out *Power Rangers* is a TV show about teenagers who, through their ability to do some mighty morphin', become superheroes. And, it turns out, Tommy was *not* in the Power Rangers.

[**] If we had a "Kill Guys with a Rubber Spatula" ministry, we would have immediately made Tommy the leader. But at that time, we lacked that particular ministry.

was afraid to.* Finally, I stopped and asked, "What are you smiling about?"

Tommy laughed and shocked everyone when he said, "We're coming with you."

They did. Tommy and his wife and two kids moved to Las Vegas to help us start the church. After years of seminary (Tommy didn't choose the one-year option like I did), Tommy would finally be a pastor.

Tommy has a Harley. (Are you surprised?) And when he arrived in Vegas, he realized that there was probably a bunch of rough-and-tumble Harley riders who wouldn't set foot in a church, so Tommy joined a biker club. Well, he said it was a club. It seemed more like a gang to me. It was a bunch of scary-looking guys who wore leather jackets and rode Harleys. If they didn't want you in their "club" anymore, they would take your leather jacket and cut it in half. I'd never heard of a club like that! So Tommy joined these guys, built relationships with them, and began sharing his faith with them. Eventually he invited the leader of the gang (I mean, "club") to our new church. The leader showed up—big, tall, ornery, and with a Wiccan girlfriend. And eventually he said yes to Jesus, and Tommy baptized him.

Tommy also has tattoos. He realized that there were more than three hundred tattoo shops in Las Vegas and more than a thousand tattoo artists, and that close to none of them

*There were no spatulas in sight, but Tommy was equipped with both of his lethal pinkies.

would set foot in a church. Tommy *really* developed a heart for these tattoo artists who felt rejected by the church.

How do you help tattoo artists to know God is for them? How do you lead them to experience God's love and move into a relationship with him? How do you get past the hard, painted exterior so you can tattoo on their hearts the gospel of God's love for those who think they're unfit?

I'm not completely sure.

But I know the strategy Jesus used.

Jesus is God. Jesus was in heaven. Jesus wanted humans to know God is for them, to experience God's love, to move into a relationship with him. So Jesus moved to earth and became a human.

My friend Tommy wanted to connect tattoo artists with God, so he decided to become a tattoo artist.

Unbelievable!

He had done all that training to become a pastor, and now he would have to do a yearlong apprenticeship at *no pay* to train to become a tattooer. He had come to the conclusion that other people could be pastors, but no one else was going to reach those tattoo artists.

Tommy started apprenticing at a local shop, where he built a relationship with a coworker named Randy. Pretty soon Randy started coming to our church, and not much later he gave his life to Christ. Tommy baptized him.

Even more people from the tattoo shop started showing up at our church.

But then there was Johnny. Johnny was a young tattoo artist,

Kate Moss skinny and covered from head to toe in ink.* Of all the people at the shop, he probably had the least interest in Tommy or in Tommy's "spirituality." Tommy was trying to figure out how he could grow their friendship. One day he asked, "Johnny, what are you into?" Johnny had to think about that for a bit. Finally he said, "I don't know, tattoos . . . and Harry Potter." Tommy told Johnny that he had never read or seen any Harry Potter stuff, which blew Johnny's mind. Tommy asked how many Harry Potter movies there were. Johnny proudly told him, "Eight, and I own them all." Tommy sighed. He didn't care to watch any of the Harry Potter movies, but he cared a lot about Johnny. He asked, "Do you want to watch them again? I'd watch them with you." Johnny was stoked.

Soon they began their marathon. Whenever there were no clients at the shop, Johnny and Tommy would sneak into the back room and continue the seemingly endless hours of watching Harry Potter.

This led, finally, to the day Johnny pushed the pause button and asked Tommy where Mother Teresa was in the Bible.

That conversation led, finally, to the day Johnny showed up at one of our church services.

That led, finally, to the day Johnny decided to say yes to Jesus and have Tommy baptize him.

Bigger Impact

For me, having a bigger impact with my life meant becoming a pastor.

---

*No joke. I'm pretty sure his eyelids are tattooed.

For Tommy, it meant no longer being a pastor.

I don't know what it will mean for you.

But I do know that God made you to make an impact.

I do know that God has put you in some places where perhaps you alone can have an impact for him.

I do know that God has put some people in your life on whom perhaps you alone can have an impact for him.

And I do know that if you pay attention, he'll lead you down a path that will allow you to have even greater impact for him.

And because of Tommy, I know this: God is for the tattooed.

8

GOD FOR THE ATHEISTS

I HAD LEARNED that God is for doubters, for people who keep finding questions creeping into their faith. That may give you a sense of relief. It might surprise you. Or it might not, since we're talking about people who *do* have faith—maybe not perfect faith, but at least they have faith.

But what about people who don't have any faith? Is God for atheists?

King David wrote that the person who believes there is no God is a fool.[1] And Paul wrote that God is angry with those who deny his existence, since he has made it obvious to everyone that there is a God.[2]

I believe all that is true.

But could it also be true that, even still, God is for the atheists?

I started the church in Virginia Beach in part to find out, and because I hoped it was true.

And I'll give you what I now believe to be the answer. It's an answer we find in the Bible, in our experiences, and (oddly) in the movie *The Count of Monte Cristo*.

Apologetics or an Apology?

Before I share with you what I would say about atheists, I want to share with you what I would say *to* an atheist. And it probably won't be what you expect. What you probably expect is apologetics, which is a defense of the Christian faith.

In fact, most people would say that what an atheist needs is apologetics, but I'd say what an atheist needs most is an apology.

Atheists need an apology because so many Christians throughout the years have done so many things that cause people to *not* believe. People look at Christians—the way we think, talk, and act—and they come to the conclusion that there's no way this Christianity deal can be real. They come to the conclusion that there's no way there's a God and *this* is what he's into. There's no way that God came to earth in the person of Jesus and died for *this*.

So while the Bible says God has given people all kinds of reasons to believe, I would say people have also been given all kinds of reasons to *not* believe. Therefore, what atheists may need, even more than apologetics, is an apology.

So in case you're an atheist, I'd like to apologize.

I apologize for the Crusades of the church in the eleventh through thirteenth centuries, when church people went out on supposed holy wars trying to take cities they believed belonged to them.

I apologize for the Inquisition, when the church would put people on trial for not having orthodox beliefs and would hand the heretics over to the government to be punished.

I apologize for people who were sent out by the church to discover the New World and ended up killing natives in the Caribbean and in South, Central, and North America. And they claimed to do it in the name of Christ.

I apologize for Christians in the southern states of the US who were racist and who tried to find ways to use the Bible to justify their support of slavery.

I apologize for televangelists we see on TV who sell God like used-car salesmen and for the priests we read about in the news who have used their religious position to commit heinous acts against innocent children.

I apologize for Christians who are trying to change the world, not through love and relationship but through politics and power, and have made Christianity seem ugly and distasteful.

I apologize for churches that through their Sunday morning services and teaching have somehow managed to make God seem irrelevant.

I apologize for churches that have turned the message of Christianity into "You have to follow the rules to be in this religion" rather than teaching the truth: that God loves you just as you are, not as you should be, and he wants to have a *relationship* with you.

I apologize for churches that make Jesus and following Jesus seem boring, when really he is the most dynamic person who ever lived, and following him is an adventure.

I apologize that so many Christians have become known for what they're against instead of what they're for. Jesus said the most important thing is to love God and love people, but there are people today who preach hate and hold up ugly signs, and I am sorry.

I know all those people say they believe in Jesus and claim they do it all in Jesus' name, but that doesn't mean it's true. Jesus talked about this.

He began by warning us, "Watch out for false prophets. They come to you in sheep's clothing, but inwardly they are ferocious wolves."[3] He was telling us to watch out for people who claim to represent him but don't.

He continued, "By their fruit you will recognize them. Do people pick grapes from thornbushes, or figs from thistles? Likewise, every good tree bears good fruit, but a bad tree bears bad fruit. A good tree cannot bear bad fruit, and a bad tree cannot bear good fruit. Every tree that does not bear good fruit is cut down and thrown into the fire. Thus, by their fruit you will recognize them."[4] The point is that you determine whether people truly represent Jesus not by whether they *say* they represent him but by the evidence of their lives. An apple tree might say it's a pear tree, but you can see the apples.

And people might say they're for Jesus, but you can see when they're not.

Jesus continued, "Not everyone who says to me, 'Lord, Lord,' will enter the kingdom of heaven, but only he who does the will of my Father who is in heaven. Many will say to me on that day, 'Lord, Lord, did we not prophesy in your name and in your name drive out demons and in your name perform many miracles?' Then I will tell them plainly, 'I never knew you. Away from me, you evildoers!'"[5] Could Jesus make it clearer than that? There will be people who, when they die, will stand before Jesus, convinced that they lived for him and did things for him. And Jesus will tell them that what they did was evil and that he never knew them.

Those people were not following Jesus when they did all that, and I'm sorry they said they were and that they gave the wrong impression of what God is like.

But I'm not done apologizing, because the problems go deeper. All that I have apologized for so far is historical and general, but I realize for many people this has become deeply personal. So more apologies are in order.

I apologize for the preacher or Sunday school teacher at your childhood church who yelled at you for running through the halls and made you feel like you couldn't be yourself there.

I apologize if you had Christian parents who used the Bible as a weapon instead of a source of encouragement and taught you that God was someone to fear instead of love.

I apologize for the uncle who kept a Bible on the coffee table and a stack of porn under his bed.

I apologize for the neighbors you heard screaming at each other throughout the week and then watched as they pulled out of their driveway every Sunday morning to go to church.

I apologize for the church that made you think you weren't good enough because you didn't have enough money to dress a certain way.

I apologize if you went to a church or to a church leader for help, and no one recognized that you were in need. Or if a Christian gave you a simplistic, clichéd answer for a complicated and sensitive question.

All those things are a perversion of what Christianity is truly about and how Christians are supposed to treat people. The Bible talks about how Christians should live godly lives of love. Jesus told his followers, "A new command I give you: Love one another. As I have loved you, so you must love one another. By this everyone will know that you are my disciples, if you love one another."[6] He said that what his followers should be known for is love.

The Bible also says Christians should be "blameless and pure, 'children of God without fault in a warped and crooked generation.' Then [they] will shine . . . like stars in the sky as [they] hold firmly to the word of life."[7]

We're told about Christians that "in every way they will make the teaching about God our Savior attractive."[8]

The people who have hurt you were not living the life of love Jesus called them to, and I'm sorry.

But I'm not done apologizing, as the trouble goes even deeper. The problem doesn't lie with just "those Christians"; it's also with *me*.

So I apologize because too often I'm insensitive. I can be judgmental. I'm not as loving as I should be.

I apologize because the Bible tells me to put my neighbor before myself, and I don't even know the names of most of my neighbors.

I apologize because Jesus tells me to feed the poor, to care for orphans and widows, and I have done very little of that.

Jesus tells us to visit prisoners and I did that . . . once.

I apologize because people see me preaching sermons about loving your enemies and praying for those who persecute you, but you wouldn't see a whole lot of that in my actual life.

The Bible says, "What good is it, my brothers and sisters, if someone claims to have faith but has no deeds? Can such faith save them? Suppose a brother or a sister is without clothes and daily food. If one of you says to them, 'Go in peace; keep warm and well fed,' but does nothing about their physical needs, what good is it? In the same way, faith by itself, if it is not accompanied by action, is dead."[9]

I really do have faith, but too often I have faith by itself. And I'm sorry.

What makes all of this so colossally sad is that it is so different from what Jesus is really like. Christians throughout the ages, sometimes including me, have given so many people the wrong impression. But Jesus really is the most loving, dynamic, passionate, compassionate, funny[10], fascinating, caring person you could ever imagine.

And when people really follow Jesus, they *are* known for love, and they do amazing things for people who are hurting, who are in need, who are marginalized.

I mean, honestly, when you look at the history of Christians and churches, yes, there are some embarrassing things that need to be apologized for because they misrepresent Jesus. But there are also so many things (actually *way more things*) that represent Jesus accurately—things that show the world what he is really like and what following him does in a person's life.

For example, in the first couple of centuries, Christianity grew like crazy, and historians tell us that a big part of the reason was *plagues*. Typically, widespread deadly epidemics don't add to any religion's membership, but historians tell us that Christianity grew rapidly in part because of two appalling plagues.* When the plagues came, everyone fled the cities to avoid the lethal contagion—everyone, that is, except Christians. Instead, they stayed and ministered to the sick and dying. A man from that time named Dionysius wrote of how the Christians responded to the plague of AD 260. He explains that they "showed unbounded love and loyalty, never sparing themselves and thinking only of one another. Heedless of danger, they took charge of the sick, attending to their every need and ministering to them in Christ, and

---

*They were seriously horrific. In some cities, two-thirds of the population died. At the peak of one of these plagues, as many as five thousand people a day were dying in Rome.

with them departed this life serenely happy; for they were infected by others with the disease, drawing on themselves the sickness of their neighbors and cheerfully accepting their pains. Many, in nursing and curing others, transferred their death to themselves and died in their stead."[11]

That's what it looks like to follow Jesus.

Or take the abolitionist movement that finally put an end to the enslavement of people of African descent in England and the United States. In 1833, slavery was abolished in England. The people* responsible for showing the British— and the world—that slavery was wrong did so because of their faith in God and their belief that we are all created in his image and therefore have inherent value. And it was the actions in England, spurred on by these men, that profoundly affected American attitudes and eventually led to the end of slavery in the United States.

In fact, although most would give the credit for ending slavery in the United States to Abraham Lincoln, Lincoln is said to have given the credit to Harriet Beecher Stowe. Her book *Uncle Tom's Cabin* helped people to understand that slavery could not continue. When Lincoln met Stowe in the midst of the Civil War, he reportedly said, "So you're the little woman who wrote the book that made this great war." Harriet Beecher Stowe was the daughter of a preacher, and all her brothers were preachers. Harriet herself placed her faith in Jesus when she was fourteen years old. She attended

---

*Like William Wilberforce, Thomas Buxton, Zachary Macaulay, and Thomas Clarkson.

seminary and later married a theology professor. About *Uncle Tom's Cabin* she said, "I wrote what I did because as a woman, as a mother I was oppressed and brokenhearted with the sorrows and injustice I saw, because as a Christian I felt the dishonor to Christianity—because as a lover of my country I trembled at the coming day of wrath."[12]

The abolition of slavery is just one example. Did you know that Christians, in the name of Christ, have founded the majority of hospitals in the world? And that the church is still the largest single provider of health care in most of the world's poorest places? And that the church leads the world in offering free health care to the terminally ill?[13]

Christians and churches have also led the way in starting programs for the poor and marginalized, such as free schooling for poor children, the world's largest orphanage system, and debt relief for the poor.

Christians have also been pioneers in foster care, social work, and campaigning for laws to protect children from abuse.

In the areas of prison reform and labor reform, the experts will tell you that it was Christ followers like John Howard and Anthony Ashley Cooper who led the way because they were trying to follow Jesus.

It was Christians who founded the 12-step programs based on biblical principles. These programs help people walk the path of healing and toward wholeness.

Christians who were motivated by Christ's love initiated programs and developments to help the handicapped, like the braille system and education for the deaf.

We see the positive impact of Christians in education as well. Many movements for world literacy were started and advanced by Christians. Efforts to educate young children, including the establishment of kindergartens, were the result of people trying to live out their faith. Churches founded 128 of the first 138 universities in America.

The Royal Society for the Prevention of Cruelty to Animals owes its start to a Christian minister.

So many of the world's philanthropic organizations are Christian—organizations like World Vision and Compassion International, which provide food and education to children with limited resources, and Habitat for Humanity, which provides homes for the poor. The Salvation Army, the YMCA, the Red Cross, and many others started as Christian initiatives by people who were trying to live out the love of Jesus.

Beyond Christian organizations, many individual Christ followers live out their faith in sacrificial and servant-hearted ways. Two-time Pulitzer Prize–winning journalist Nicholas Kristof, a regular columnist for the *New York Times*—who is not a Christian—writes, "Evangelicals are disproportionately likely to donate 10 percent of their incomes to charities, mostly church-related. More important, go to the front lines, at home or abroad, in the battles against hunger, malaria, prison rape, obstetric fistula, human trafficking or genocide, and some of the bravest people you meet are evangelical Christians (or conservative Catholics, similar in many ways) who truly live their faith."[14]

In his book *Vanishing Grace*, Philip Yancey writes about the findings of sociologist Robert Putnam: "Robert Putnam, author of the groundbreaking book *Bowling Alone*, documents that religious Americans are more likely to give money to a homeless person, return excess change to a shop clerk, donate blood, help a sick neighbor with shopping or housework, spend time with someone who is depressed, offer a seat to a stranger, or help someone find a job. Regular church attenders give almost four times as much money to charity as their secular neighbors and twice as many of them do volunteer work among the poor, the infirm, or the elderly."[15]

Most people would say what an atheist needs is apologetics, but I'd say what an atheist needs most is an apology for the hypocritical way so many alleged Christians have lived out their supposed faith.

At the same time, I'd encourage atheists to take a closer look at the amazing way so many authentic Christians have succeeded in living out their loving and compassionate faith.

And I would challenge Christians, including myself, to understand that we represent Jesus. Most people will never read the Bible and see who Jesus truly is. Instead, they just look at us. So we need to live a life of love as he did and make the teaching about God our Savior attractive.

Is God for Atheists?

So now, let's get back to our original question: Is God for atheists?

There's a scene in the movie *The Count of Monte Cristo*

where this guy gets put in prison. When he goes in, he believes in God, but after years of feeling alone and being confused by his circumstances, he loses his faith. Later in prison he meets an old priest who asks him where he's at with God. And the man says, "I don't believe in God anymore." The old priest looks him in the eye and says, "That's okay. He still believes in you."

If you're an atheist, I want to tell you that God still believes in you. God is still for you.

And in our church in Virginia Beach we saw hundreds of people who had given up on God discover that God had never given up on them.

If you're a Christian, you may wonder if I'm right about all this.

What about the verse that says people who believe there is no God are fools? Yeah, that's in there. And it's true. People who don't believe in God are fools. But does that mean God isn't for them?

What about the verse that says God feels wrath toward those who deny his existence? Yeah, that's in there too. And it's true. People who don't believe in God are under the wrath of God. But does that mean God isn't for them?

Can you feel anger, even wrath, toward someone and still be for that person, still love that person? Of course you can.

Think of your kids. As a parent, there will be times when you are angry with your kids. They did something wrong. In your gut, you may feel wrath. But you still love and are for them.

My mother was a schoolteacher. In 1993, one of her thirteen-year-old students, Eric Smith, murdered a four-year-old boy. It made national news, and everyone was furious with him. *Everyone* was angry, including his parents. In televised interviews soon after the murder, Eric's mother expressed her horror at her son's crime. But she said, at the same time, that she couldn't stop loving him. No matter what he did, she would always love him. Of course—he was her kid.

God is outraged by our sins. He's angry at people who deny his existence. But we're not just sinners, and an atheist isn't just an atheist. God wants us all to be his children, and an atheist still has the opportunity to say yes and be adopted as God's kid.

That's why God doesn't give up on us. As the Bible says, "The Lord is not slow in keeping his promise, as some understand slowness. Instead he is patient with you, not wanting anyone to perish, but everyone to come to repentance."[16] Did you notice it *doesn't* say, "God is patient with everyone, except the atheists"? Did you notice it *doesn't* say, "God does want the atheists to perish"? No. God does not want *anyone* to perish and wants *everyone* to come to repentance.

To repent means to turn around, to change direction. Jesus gives us a good picture of that repentant turning in the story of the Prodigal Son who decides to turn around and go home. God wants everyone to come to repentance. He's inviting everyone to come home.

So the ball is in the court of the atheist.

As the saying goes, God is a gentleman and does not force

himself on anyone. If an atheist persists in stubborn disbelief and chooses to leave God out of his life, God will honor that. As the Bible says, "If you seek him, he will be found by you, but if you forsake him, he will forsake you."[17]

But this doesn't mean God is giving up. He's inviting every atheist to come home. A long time ago he said to people who had turned away from him, "'You will seek me and find me when you seek me with all your heart. I will be found by you,' declares the LORD, 'and will bring you back from captivity. I will gather you from all the nations and places where I have banished you,' declares the LORD, 'and will bring you back to the place from which I carried you into exile.'"[18]

God is inviting everyone, including atheists, to seek him. When they do, they find him.

An Atheist Comes Home

Antony Flew was a highly influential atheist. A man named Roy Abraham Varghese wrote, "It is not too much to say that within the last hundred years, no mainstream philosopher has developed the kind of systematic, comprehensive, original, and influential exposition of atheism that is to be found in Antony Flew's fifty years of theological writings."[19]

Antony Flew was the spokesperson for atheism for fifty years, but to his credit he was open to the idea that maybe he hadn't looked at all the evidence. So he continued to think. He continued to study. And he continued to look at questions like . . .

Where do the laws of nature come from? We take it for granted that there are laws that are constant and seem to govern the universe. Water will boil tomorrow at the same temperature as it does today. Gravity always works the same way. But this troubles philosophers and scientists. Why do these constant laws of nature exist? Why are they the same today as they were yesterday? If there are constant laws, then something must impose them on the universe. Antony Flew came to the conclusion that the best and probably only option is that there is a God who created and imposed these laws in our universe.

He also asked, *Why is the world perfectly designed for life?* The idea that our world and the laws of nature seem to be perfectly crafted to bring about and sustain life is called the *anthropic principle* or fine-tuning argument. For life to exist, the speed of light, the gravitational constant, and the strength of the weak and strong nuclear forces all have to fall within very specific parameters. A brilliant guy named Tim Keller writes, "The probability of this perfect calibration happening by chance is so tiny as to be statistically negligible."[20]

Even atheistic scientist Stephen Hawking has to agree. He writes, "The odds against a universe like ours emerging out of something like the Big Bang are enormous. I think there are clearly religious implications. . . . It would be very difficult to explain why the universe should have begun in just this way, except as the act of a God who intended to create beings like us."[21] Antony Flew began to come to this conclusion as well.

Flew also wondered, *Why does life exist at all?* True, all the conditions of our world are favorable for life to exist, but that still doesn't explain how life itself originated. So how do we account for the origin of life? According to Nobel Prize–winning physiologist George Wald, "We choose to believe the impossible: that life arose spontaneously by chance."[22] But even he, later, came to the conclusion that life must be the result of an infinitely intelligent, preexisting Mind. And Flew came to the conclusion that "it's simply absurd to suggest that the more elaborate feat of the origin of life could have been achieved by chance."[23]

And then there was the question, *How could something come from nothing?* Scientists talk about the world starting from a big bang. Flew wrote, "If the universe had a beginning, it became entirely sensible, almost inevitable, to ask what produced this beginning."[24] He says the existence of the universe begs an explanation. There's a scientist named Francis Collins who said, "We have this very solid conclusion that the universe had an origin, the Big Bang. Fifteen billion years ago, the universe began with an unimaginably bright flash of energy from an infinitesimally small point. That implies that before that, there was nothing. I can't imagine how nature, in this case the universe, could have created itself. And the very fact that the universe had a beginning implies that someone was able to begin it."[25] He's saying that there just has to be a creator. If there was a big bang, someone had to set it off.

Flew asked questions like that, and there were many other

critical questions he didn't get to. For instance, why do we have an innate sense of right and wrong? Evolution wouldn't put that in us. If there is no God, then there is no right and wrong. You might say something's wrong, or your culture might, but I (or my culture) might say it's right. And why is your view better? Without a God, there's no standard to which we can appeal. Without God there can be no morality. But we *do* have morality; we do believe there's right and wrong.

Antony Flew reexamined some important questions and decided that his original conclusion wasn't right. And he shocked the world by writing a book called *There Is a God: How the World's Most Notorious Atheist Changed His Mind.*

The atheist repented.

And God's invitation to every atheist is to turn around and come home.

9

GOD FOR THE WORRIERS

YEARS AGO I came across a book called *Foreign Bodies* by Hwee Hwee Tan. It's a novel about three friends who struggle with different problems.

One of the characters, a girl from Singapore named Mei, describes how her grandfather died because he had a foreign body, a fish bone, inside him that no one ever detected. The doctors saw the external symptoms—gangrene in his fingers and toes—and tried to fix them, but they never detected or dealt with the true problem, the fish bone inside him.

Mei realizes that the issues she and her two friends deal with aren't the real problems; they're just external symptoms resulting from a foreign body inside. Not literally, of course, but it's like there's something inside Mei and her friends that's not supposed to be there. And she wonders: What's the real problem behind the problem?

Soon after I read that book, my wife became very sick. She started throwing up a lot. In fact, one week she probably vomited sixty times. When that happens, you know something's wrong, because getting sick that many times is not normal. If you looked at her life, at her behavior from the outside, you would have thought her problem was all the vomiting. And that's true, but it was just a *symptom* of the problem. The real cause was that she was pregnant. And her body didn't respond well to the presence of that foreign body inside her. Because of that, she was throwing up.[1]

While she was throwing up, I was worrying about her. When that happens, you know something is wrong, because worry is not normal. It's so common that we accept it as if it were, but we were not meant to worry. Just like a gangrene in your fingers and toes, or throwing up sixty times in a week, worry is a sign that something is wrong. There is a foreign body inside us.

You may be thinking, *Really? In a book about pimps and prostitutes and atheists, you're going after worriers? Sure, I worry sometimes, but is it really a big deal?*

Yes, it is.

It's a big deal because of the external effect it has on us, but much more because of the foreign body it reveals *in* us.

Worry has very negative effects on us. The word *worry*

originated from an old Anglo-Saxon verb meaning "to choke or to strangle." And that's what worry does.

It can choke or strangle you *physically*. Did you know that around 30 percent of all deaths are heart related,[2] and many of those are brought on by high blood pressure and anxiety, both of which stem from worry? During the 1970s, the most prescribed drug was Valium, which is used to treat anxiety. Then Valium was bypassed by Tagamet, a breakthrough medical treatment for ulcers.

Worry also chokes and strangles us *emotionally*. We've all felt the heaviness of worrying about the what-ifs.

A mother sits up at night worrying, *What if my daughter keeps going down the wrong path?*

A son lies awake in bed at night worrying, *What if I don't make the team? Will my dad still love me?*

A man sits in fear at his desk every day worrying, *What if there's another round of layoffs?*

A teenager walks nervously into the school cafeteria every day worrying, *What if I can never get anyone to like me?*

A single girl sits alone on another Friday night worrying, *What if I never meet the right guy? What if I come home to an empty house every night for the rest of my life?*

The stress of it all is debilitating. Worry smothers the emotional life right out of us.

Worry can also choke and strangle us *spiritually*. Jesus once told a story about a farmer who went out and planted seed, most of which didn't survive. Jesus described various reasons for this and said, "Other seed fell among thorns, which grew up and choked the plants."[3] Later, when people asked him, "What were you talking about?" Jesus explained that it was a metaphor. He said, "The seed falling among the thorns refers to someone who hears the word, but the worries of this life and the deceitfulness of wealth choke the word, making it unfruitful."[4] Make sure you get this: Jesus said that worrying could choke the spiritual life right out of you.

So, yeah, it really is a big deal.

But again, the main reason it's a big deal isn't because of the external effect it has on us but because of the foreign body it reveals *in* us.

In the last chapter we considered whether God is for the atheists, for people who deny his existence. I think so. For me, the more troubling question is whether God is for the people that author Craig Groeschel calls "Christian atheists"[5]—people who claim Jesus but live like there is no God. There's something significantly worse about being a Christian atheist than about being a regular, garden-variety atheist. Why? Think of it this way: if I'm not faithful to a woman I've never made a commitment to, that's one thing. But if I'm not faithful to a woman I've vowed to be faithful to? Yikes. And for atheists to act like there is no God, that's one thing. The Bible calls that foolishness. But for a *Christian* to act like there is no God? Yikes. As we've already seen, the Bible calls that adultery. And that's worse.

So how might a Christian live like an atheist? Our minds might turn to some ugly, blatant sin. But let's go with one of the most common and obvious ways we live as Christian atheists—worrying.

One time Jesus sat down to teach. The crowd didn't realize it, but this would become probably his most famous teaching. Today we call it the Sermon on the Mount. One of the main topics was . . . worry. (Apparently Jesus thought it was a pretty big deal.) Jesus taught this:

> No one can serve two masters. Either you will hate the one and love the other, or you will be devoted to the one and despise the other. You cannot serve both God and money.
>
> Therefore I tell you, *do not worry* about your life, what you will eat or drink; or about your body, what you will wear. Is not life more than food, and the body more than clothes? Look at the birds of the air; they do not sow or reap or store away in barns, and yet your heavenly Father feeds them. Are you not much more valuable than they? Can any one of you by worrying add a single hour to your life?
>
> And why do you worry about clothes? See how the flowers of the field grow. They do not labor or spin. Yet I tell you that not even Solomon in all his splendor was dressed like one of these. If that is how God clothes the grass of the field, which is here today and tomorrow is thrown into the fire, will he not much more clothe you—you of little faith? So *do not worry*, saying, "What shall we eat?" or "What

shall we drink?" or "What shall we wear?" For the pagans run after all these things, and your heavenly Father knows that you need them. But seek first his kingdom and his righteousness, and all these things will be given to you as well. Therefore *do not worry* about tomorrow, for tomorrow will worry about itself. Each day has enough trouble of its own.[6]

Repeatedly Jesus said, "Do not worry."

What exactly did Jesus mean? Well, I think it's important to understand there's a difference between concern and worry.

Concern focuses on probable difficulties and results in action. Concern is *I have a big test and it's going to be difficult. I'd better study for it.* Or *My brakes are going bad. It's going to cost $500 to replace them; I'd better start saving some money.*

Worry focuses on circumstances that are beyond our control and results in inaction. It's been said that worrying is mentally living through a crisis before it arrives.

In the Sermon on the Mount, Jesus not only tells us not to worry, but he also reveals some of the sources of our worries. Jesus was speaking two thousand years ago, but it's fascinating how little things have changed.

The first source of worry that Jesus identifies is money. Jesus had previously been speaking about how our faith shouldn't be in material possessions and that we should seek treasure in heaven, not on earth. He concludes by saying, "You cannot serve both God and money. Therefore I tell you, do not worry." It's still true today that finances are one of the most common sources of worry. The bills seem to outweigh the paychecks. You finally get ahead, and then you're hit by another setback. Financial stress can ruin a day, a marriage, even a life. You might think, *Exactly! That's why I need more money! If I had more, I'd worry less.* But that's not true. People with more just have more to worry about. And Jesus says, "Don't worry." Don't worry about finances.

Another source of worry Jesus mentions is food. He says, "I tell you, do not worry about your life, what you will eat or drink." In Jesus' day, people's worry about food was whether they'd have any at all. Hunger is still a problem all over the world. And where there is enough food, many of us starve ourselves and suffer from eating disorders, while others suffer from health problems caused by eating too much. But Jesus says, "Don't worry about food."

A third source of worry Jesus points out is fashion. Jesus says, "Do not worry . . . about your body, what you will wear. Is not life more than food, and the body more than clothes?" In that day, people were probably worrying about whether they'd be able to clothe their families adequately. For some today, that's still a pressing problem. In our society, though, most people aren't concerned with having clothes but with having the *right* clothes. Am I overdressed? Underdressed? Should I buy that dress? Do these pants make my butt look fat? Or does my butt make these pants look fat? But Jesus says, "Don't worry about what you wear."

Then Jesus points out a fourth source of worry, the future.

He says, "Can any one of you by worrying add a single hour to your life?" and "Don't worry about tomorrow." It's tempting to worry about the future because it's so uncertain. But even when we worry, still the only thing certain about the future is the uncertainty of it. And the more you worry about the future of your life, the less quality of life you're going to have today. So Jesus says, "Do not worry about tomorrow."

Why does Jesus make such a big deal about worrying?

Jesus addresses that when he says, "Look at the birds of the air; they do not sow or reap or store away in barns, and yet your heavenly Father feeds them. Are you not much more valuable than they?" Worry assumes that God will not provide for me. It imagines that God cares for the birds more than he cares for me.

And Jesus says, "Do not worry, saying, 'What shall we eat?' or 'What shall we drink?' or 'What shall we wear?' For the pagans run after all these things, and your heavenly Father knows that you need them." Jesus says that when we worry, we're acting like pagans. What's a pagan? A person who doesn't know God.

Jesus is basically saying, "It makes sense for pagans to worry, because they don't know God. They don't believe they have a heavenly Father to take care of them. But it *doesn't* make sense for believers to worry, because they *do* know God. They *do* have a heavenly Father to take care of them."

Do you see the fish bone? Do you see the foreign body behind worry? It's Christian atheism—living like a nonbeliever.

And when we leave God out, we have to step in. We need

someone to be in charge, someone to take care of everything, so if we won't trust God to do it, *we* have to. We take on God's job description.

No wonder we worry! We can't do what God can do. Oh, we're trying. We put all our effort into it. But it's not happening. Our plan isn't working right. The details aren't working out. And so . . . we worry.

I'll confess that, although I'm a Christian (and even a pastor), I still astound myself with my propensity for living like I don't believe in God and trying to take his place.

Like back when my wife was throwing up nonstop. She spent weeks in the hospital. We had to pay lots of money for that. She came home with a special IV called a PICC line—a long, spaghettilike tube that was inserted into her upper arm and then strung through a vein near her heart to feed and nourish her.

She wasn't throwing up anymore, but she was feeling *very* sick. She also had a superhigh temperature, so she went back to the hospital, where they discovered yeast in her blood. Tests determined that the fever and the yeast weren't the problems. They were *symptoms* of the problem. The problem was an infection in Jen's PICC line. The doctor told her, "Jen, whenever you introduce a foreign object into the human body, there are risks involved, and there can be consequences."* So Jen spent more time in the hospital. And there were more bills to pay.

---

*And I said, "I just read a book called *Foreign Bodies*—that's cool!" And he looked at me like I needed to shut up. So I shut up.

And I lived like an atheist. Instead of believing in and trusting God, I worried. *What's going to happen to my wife? What if she doesn't get better? What if all this affects the baby? What if we can't pay the bills? What if we never get out of this debt?* Instead of letting God be God in that situation, I tried to be God and take over the situation.

Jesus says that instead of living like atheists, we should live like birds. Birds live in a state of trust. That doesn't mean they sit around in their nests waiting for God to drop food into their laps.* Birds get up early. They go out looking for food. They spend lots of time looking for food. And they find food. You've heard it said, "You eat like a bird." Did you know birds eat two to three times their body weight in food every day? If we did that, we'd be eating three hundred to four hundred pounds of food a day!**

Birds work hard, but then they relax. You never hear birds chirping at night. That's because they're asleep. They're not up worrying about how many worms will be out there the next day or if there might be a bug shortage. They instinctively know they'll be taken care of.

The solution for worry is trust. We need to learn to trust God, to live like he really exists, and to let him be God in our lives. When we worry, it shows that we don't really trust him. When he says he'll take care of us, we don't believe he's telling the truth. But God can be trusted.

So we can leave God's job description to God, and we

---

*Actually, I don't think birds have laps. But you know what I mean.
**I've tried it. It's miserable.

can just do our job. But what *is* our job? Jesus tells us in this teaching: "Put God's kingdom first. Do what he wants you to do. Then all those things will also be given to you."[7] Our job is to put God first in our lives. And then, Jesus says, we won't have to worry about all these other things, because God will give them to us as well.

When we put God first, we'll learn to trust him, and we'll stop worrying. We'll learn to live one day at a time. That's how Jesus concludes: "Therefore do not worry about tomorrow, for tomorrow will worry about itself. Each day has enough trouble of its own."[8] Jesus is like, "There's always going to be plenty to worry about. But you don't need to, because you are not a pagan; you know God."

The Two Questions

Really, I think all of this comes down to answering two questions.

First question: *Do you know that your heavenly Father knows?* Jesus said, "Don't worry," and that means it's possible for us not to worry. The reason it's possible is that you have a God who knows what you need and will take care of you.

That doesn't mean everything will always end up okay and your life will be perfect and problem-free. But it *does* mean that you have a heavenly Father who knows, and no matter what happens, you can trust him.

Second question: *Do you know your heavenly Father?* Jesus is saying your heavenly Father knows, but do you know your heavenly Father? Because, remember, the solution for stress is trust.

If you don't really know God, you can't have the level of trust you need. If I told you to never worry again but instead to trust my uncle Stan, that would be a struggle for you because you don't know my uncle Stan. In the same way, if you don't really know God, if you don't have an intimate relationship with your heavenly Father, you won't be able to trust him in a way that allows you to stop worrying.

When I first encountered the idea of God, I didn't believe at all. But studying the evidence for the Bible and Jesus led me to believe. At that point I knew *about* God, but I still didn't really *know him*.

I studied the evidence for the Bible and Jesus, and the evidence led me to believe. Little by little, as my relationship with God grows, I'm increasingly able to trust more and worry less. I still have a ways to go. But the closer I get to fully trusting God, the better my life is. And I want to totally get there.

I told you about how my wife got sick during her pregnancy but not about the problems we experienced post-delivery. The day after my son, Dawson, was born, he had a high temperature and was dehydrated. The doctors feared meningitis and potential heart complications. For seven days we remained in the hospital as they watched him closely and ran a battery of tests. And I did a lot of worrying.

Finally, on a Tuesday afternoon, they gave him a clean bill of health and sent us home. Wednesday afternoon, my wife was lying on our couch with a high temperature, freezing with chills, and shaking uncontrollably. Thursday morning she was readmitted to the hospital with a mysterious uterine infection and a 104.7 degree fever. The nurses got her temperature down, but she and Dawson spent the next five days back in the hospital together. The doctors couldn't figure out what was wrong. And I continued to worry.

One night, Jen's temperature shot back up over 104 degrees. She was shaking so much it was like she was vibrating. As a nurse tried to get the fever down, I stared at the scene in front of me, thinking, *What is happening? There's nothing I can do!*

Finally, Jen's temperature came down a little, and the nurse left. Jen turned to me and said, "I know I'm going to be okay."

I asked her, "Why? How can you know that?"

"Because," she answered, "while all that was happening, I was singing a song to God, and he just kind of let me know he's here and that he loves us." I asked what she had been singing. And she sang it. She was still shaking as she sang a song by a guy named Rich Mullins: "Hold me Jesus, 'cause I'm shaking like a leaf. You have been King of my glory; won't you be my Prince of Peace?"

That's the kind of trust I want. I'm guessing it's what you want as well. When we get there, we'll live without worry.

It turned out that the reason my wife had all those problems was that she had a foreign body in her. During the delivery, a tiny fragment of the placenta stayed in her, and her body was attacking it. Everything she experienced were the symptoms resulting from that foreign body.

Worry is a symptom of a foreign body. If we address the foreign body, we can live a life without worry.

We don't have to be God. We have a heavenly Father who knows, and we can know our heavenly Father. And our heavenly Father is for us, even if we've been worrying like Christian atheists.

10

GOD FOR SIN CITY

AFTER TWELVE YEARS of doing ministry in and loving Virginia Beach, my wife and I felt God prompting us to start another church, this time in Las Vegas. Originally, we backed away from the challenge. We didn't want to move and start all over again from scratch. But God kept confirming the crazy call to start a church for people who worked on and lived around the Las Vegas Strip. And considering all the damage my father had done in Sin City, it seemed like just the kind of poetic story of redemption God would write.

We moved to Sin City.

I came up with an idea for a book: *My Year in Las Vegas.* I thought, *Las Vegas is fascinating. Starting a church in the*

middle of Sin City should be interesting. I can tell about the
cool things that happen, the crazy things that happen, and how
I tried to love the city and its people and let them know about
God's love.

I told the publisher I had at the time, and they said no.
I was surprised and disappointed. When I asked why, they
explained that Christians would not buy a book about "Sin
City." I was told it would be considered a "brown paper bag"
book—the kind of book someone would be embarrassed to
walk out of a store holding. Christians don't want anything
to do with a city famous for sin, and if for some reason they
did buy the book, they'd be embarrassed if their friends knew.
They would prefer to pretend Sin City doesn't exist.

And I started to wonder: *Why* does *Sin City exist? What
made Sin City, Sin City?*

It began the way sin always does, with a desperate search
for water.* In 1829, a Mexican trading party veered off the
Spanish Trail on their way to Los Angeles. They set up camp
and sent people out to search for water. Rafael Rivera left the
group and set off alone into the arid wasteland. Two weeks
later he discovered a spring of water in the middle of the
desert. There was actually grass there. That oasis eventually
became the location of Las Vegas, and that grass gave the city
its name: Las Vegas means "the meadows."

Fourteen years after Rivera first came across the spring,
explorer John C. Fremont camped there while on a map-

---

*Just hold that thought; it will make sense later.

making expedition. Once the spring was literally on the map, it quickly became a popular stopping place for people heading west to California. Railroad developers realized that Las Vegas was the perfect location for a train stop and a town surrounding it.

Finally, in 1905, Las Vegas was officially founded as a city. Gambling quickly became a problem, and so on midnight, October 1, 1910, the Nevada government declared gambling illegal. Secret backroom games sprang up all over town, followed by speakeasies.

In 1931, Las Vegas exploded with growth due to the start of construction on the Hoover Dam project. The project employed up to five thousand people at a time, and thousands more came to the city looking for work on the dam. The population of Las Vegas grew from five thousand to over twenty-five thousand almost overnight. A *huge* majority of the residents were men. This created an exploding market for entertainment for those men. It also created an exploding market for women to entertain those men. This led to even more illegal gambling, saloons, and showgirl theaters. The state of Nevada soon realized they were licked, that gambling would remain a major source of spending by the dam workers. Nevada was mired in the Great Depression, so in 1931, working under the "If you can't beat 'em, tax 'em" philosophy, Nevada legalized gambling. And Las Vegas, already with an established gambling industry, began its quick ascent to its status as the gambling capital of the world.

By the 1950s, more than eight million people were visiting

Las Vegas every year to watch entertainers like Elvis Presley and Frank Sinatra and to try their luck with slot machines and strippers. Now that number is closer to forty million.

And that brings us to present-day Las Vegas, a town that more than ten thousand strippers call home. A place where there are billboards with porn casting calls—"Make $500 by starring in an adult video today!"—and even the billboards for *dentists* feature half-naked girls. A city that has newspaper stands *everywhere* with catalogs of girls you can have "In Your Room in Twenty Minutes!" A place with the highest suicide rate and one of the highest crime rates in the nation. A city that employs three times as many police officers as any other city its size. One that has been called a "modern amalgamation of Sodom, Gomorrah, and Hell."[1] Las Vegas is the world's city of sin.

The City That Was Sin City before Las Vegas Was Sin City

Thousands of years before Las Vegas, there was a city called Nineveh, which was known for sin. We read about Nineveh in the book of Jonah. "The word of the LORD came to Jonah son of Amittai: 'Go to the great city of Nineveh and preach against it, because its wickedness has come up before me.'"[2]

God called Jonah to go preach to the people of Nineveh. Jonah would get to share God's truth and his offer of forgiveness of sin with people who needed to hear it. What a great honor for Jonah!

What did Jonah do with this responsibility? "Jonah ran

away from the LORD and headed for Tarshish. He went down to Joppa, where he found a ship bound for that port. After paying the fare, he went aboard and sailed for Tarshish to flee from the LORD."[3]

Jonah went to the local "Anywhere but Nineveh Travel Agency" and said, "Oh? No tickets to Nineveh? Too bad! I guess I'll have to go somewhere else," and he bought a ticket to Tarshish.

God asked Jonah to go to Nineveh, which was about five hundred miles northeast from where he lived; the town of Tarshish was about thirteen hundred miles to the west. At the time, that was as far west as a person could go. Jonah was trying to run as far away as possible.

Why? Because, just as many Christians today do with Las Vegas, Jonah judged Nineveh for its sin. It's ironic. It's only from God that we learn that there are standards of right and wrong and that sin is falling short of those standards. Jonah held Nineveh to God's standards, *but* he lacked God's compassion for people who didn't live up to God's standards.

So many Christians today do the same thing. They don't offer grace because they lack the compassion to see beyond the person's sin, to see what's driving the person to sin. They forget that without grace, we're *all* in big trouble.

You've probably heard the story. Jonah got on this boat for Tarshish. A wild storm arose. All the sailors were terrified. They were experienced sailors and had seen storms, but this one was different, and they realized, "We're gonna die!"

While they were panicking, Jonah was sleeping. Think about that. Jonah was rebelling directly against the heart of God, yet somehow he was totally at peace with it. He was sleeping while everyone around him was about to die.

Again, so many Christians today are just like that. People all around us are living without God; death is coming at them like a freight train. People will face an eternity without God, but we're very comfortable. We may be a little concerned about whether our kid makes the soccer team, where we'll go on vacation next year, and how our retirement fund is doing, but for the most part, we're very comfortable. We're sleeping on the boat while everyone around us is about to go down.

So the other sailors were horrified, but Jonah was asleep. The crew started praying to any god they could think of, but Jonah didn't pray. He didn't seek God. He didn't fear God. He just continued to sleep.

The truth is that believers who run from God's mission end up living like hypocrites, just like Jonah. And just like in his story, others end up paying a price for our disobedience as well.

Finally, the other men woke Jonah up and asked him what they should do. Jonah said, "Just pick me up and throw me overboard. I'm the reason this is happening. Just kill me, and you'll be fine."[4]

Jonah was basically saying, "I would rather die than go tell those Ninevites about God," because the other option was to turn the boat around and take him back so he could obey God by going to Nineveh. But no, Jonah preferred to be thrown overboard and die rather than do that.

The sailors finally agreed with Jonah's plan and threw him into the sea. The storm immediately subsided. Jonah hit the water, and "the LORD provided a huge fish to swallow Jonah, and Jonah was in the belly of the fish three days and three nights."[5]

I realize when some of us hear that we think, *Who came up with this one? I'm supposed to believe that someone was really swallowed by a fish, lived inside of it, and then got spit out, still alive, three days later?*

Ordinarily, I would agree. But there's nothing ordinary about God. After all, if there is a God, he can do whatever he wants. If God wants to, if God needs to make a point, he can create a fish as big as he wants, command it to swallow Jonah or anyone else he wants, and keep that person alive in there as long as he wants. If there's a God, that wouldn't even be hard for him.[*]

In the huge fish, God got through to Jonah.[6] Finally Jonah realized his mistake and cried out to God. God caused the huge fish to spit him out. Jonah ended up on dry land and had a second chance.

In fact, chapter 3 of Jonah starts out, "Then the word of the LORD came to Jonah *a second time*: 'Go to the great city of Nineveh and proclaim to it the message I give you.'"[7] God

---

[*]The verse could say, "God provided a great ocean hamster to swallow Jonah," and if there's a God, that wouldn't be hard for him either. The question isn't whether a man can live in a big fish for three days (or a big hamster); the question is whether there's a God who has an interest in and intervenes in human affairs. If so, anything is possible.

wanted to give the people of Nineveh a second chance. He came to Jonah a second time to give him a second chance to share God's grace with the Ninevites.

God wants to give the people of Las Vegas a second chance. That's why I moved here.

God wants to give the people at your office a second chance. That's why he put you in that workplace.

God wants to give the people at your school a second chance. That's why he placed you in that school.

God wants to give the people in your neighborhood a second chance. That's why you live in that neighborhood.

And God wants to give you a second chance to share his grace with them. If you claim Jesus but have not been sharing him, you are living in as much rebellion against God as any sinner you could point at. But God is still for you, and right now the word of the Lord is coming to you a second time to "go" and to "proclaim to it the message I give you."

Jonah was finally going to obey. "Jonah began by going a day's journey into the city, proclaiming, 'Forty more days and Nineveh will be overthrown.'"[8] Later in this book we learn that though Jonah obeyed God and warned the Ninevites, his attitude did not change, and his heart was not in it. Did you notice that his message focused on the consequences for the Ninevites' sins and not on God's gracious offer that they could avoid those consequences by turning to him for forgiveness?

Because of the power of God and of God's message,

and despite Jonah's lack of passion and persuasiveness, "the Ninevites believed God. A fast was proclaimed, and all of them, from the greatest to the least, put on sackcloth."[9] Soon even the king of Nineveh repented and called out to God.

The people responded. But would God forgive them? Was God *really* for Nineveh?

Before you answer that question, you may need to know more about Nineveh. History records that the Ninevites would regularly bury people alive. In fact, they were known to skin people alive. They would impale their enemies on sharp poles and leave them hanging in the sun to suffer and die. They would also take people and boil them in tar.

So could God forgive even the Ninevites? "When God saw what they did and how they turned from their evil ways, he relented and did not bring on them the destruction he had threatened."[10]

Yep.

God was for and could forgive even the Ninevites.

Think about who was saved. They hadn't known God at all. Their theology was completely wrong. They were considered the most sinful people on earth, but it didn't matter, because when they had their chance, they chose to love God.

And think about Jonah. He *did* know God. His theology was right. But it didn't matter, because when he had his chance, he *didn't* have love.

God forgave Nineveh. So, can God forgive Las Vegas, the city that's a "modern day amalgamation of Sodom, Gomorrah, and Hell"? Yes.

If God can forgive those who bury people alive, he can forgive those who bury their own lives in drugs and alcohol.

If God can forgive those who skin people alive, he can forgive those who bare their skin for money.

If God can forgive those who impale their enemies and leave them hanging in the sun, he can forgive those who take the money of tourists and leave them drowning in their own debt.

God forgave Nineveh. God can forgive Las Vegas. And God can forgive your coworkers, neighbors, and family members who are far from God. No matter who they are. No matter where they've been. No matter what they've done. That's the beauty of God's grace. When you say yes to it, you don't get what you deserve. You get the opposite. It's not about your very imperfect life; it's about God's perfect love. When people say yes to God, his grace wins out over their sin every single time.

Go Proclaim the Message

God can forgive the Ninevites in your life, but for that to happen they have to say yes to his offer. To say yes to his offer, they need to know about his offer. To be made aware of his offer, they need you to share it with them.

Just like with Jonah, God has told us to go and to proclaim the message.[11]

And just like Jonah, we are living in rebellion against God if we don't proclaim the message.

The way we go about it should *not* be the same as Jonah's way.

His heart wasn't in it. We should have a passion burning inside us for all God's children to come home.

Jonah preached a message of hell and condemnation. We will *not* be effective if we do the same.

A few years ago I co-led a session at a church conference with a pastor named Cal Jernigan. Our topic was "Preaching to the Unconvinced." The format was that Cal would speak for twenty minutes, then I would speak for twenty minutes, then we would have a twenty-minute question-and-answer time. Cal walked up to the podium. I had never met him and was curious as to what he would say. He talked about how people who don't have faith in Jesus need to know you like them before they'll listen to what you have to say. He then explained that in most churches you're asked to behave. "If you're going to hang out with us you need to behave! You need to stop sinning and act like we do!" Then you're asked to believe. Once you do all that, then finally you can belong. He said that his church has reversed the order. First you belong. As soon as you show up, you'll be accepted and befriended. Then the hope is that you'll grow to believe. And his church expects people to behave only after they believe. He said, "You have to accept and befriend people first, while they're still messed up and not behaving."

I thought he did a great job, and he pretty much stole my thunder because I was going to offer the same ideas in my twenty minutes. Cal sat down; I walked up to the podium and explained that Jesus didn't make people feel worse about themselves. He made them feel loved. Jesus knew a secret that today's Christians seem to have lost: it's *love* that turns a life around. I pointed out Bible verses that say it's God's love that leads people to salvation. It seemed like everyone agreed with that. I also pointed out verses that say it's God's love that leads people to repentance. That seemed to surprise people a little. I think we believe that we go to God because of his love, but we stop sinning for fear of punishment. That's not what the Bible says. I read Titus 2:11-12: "The grace of God has appeared that offers salvation to all people. It teaches us to say 'No' to ungodliness and worldly passions, and to live self-controlled, upright and godly lives in this present age." This verse says it's the *grace* of God that teaches us to say no to ungodliness. I also showed them Romans 2:4: "Do you show contempt for the riches of his kindness, forbearance and patience, not realizing that God's kindness is intended to lead you to repentance?" I said that we must lead with love. We should present truth, and people are open to truth, but not truth from a jerk. If we lead with love, it will open people up to what we have to say. I smiled and sat down.

Cal went back to the podium and introduced the question-and-answer time. A bunch of easy questions came in, and Cal answered all of them. That didn't bother me. I figured he had more experience and wisdom to share, and I was learning from his answers.

Then a big guy with a red-as-a-tomato face and a trucker hat on his huge head stood up in the back of the room.[*]

---

[*]The trucker hat is probably not relevant, but maybe it is. And I like to include lots of details.

The guy started yelling. "You know what?" His volume kept getting louder, and his face kept getting redder. "I hear you guys talking about how you like sinners, and how you love sinners! But what I want to know is: When do you call sin, sin? When do you tell sinners that they're sinners? When do you preach about sin and hell?"

I started to breathe a sigh of relief that Cal had decided to do the entire question-and-answer time himself. Then I heard him say, "That is a great question, and Vince has a great answer for you," as he walked away from the podium and sat down.

Great.

I stood up, went to the podium, and said, "Sir, I appreciate your question, but I would encourage you, instead of assuming, to go to our website and listen to our sermons, and you tell me if I preach about sin and hell. In fact, all you have to do is listen to our sermon from this past Sunday, and you'll see that I do preach about sin and hell.* But let me ask you a question: When you read the Gospels, when do you see Jesus going up and calling sinners, sinners? When does that happen? Or do we see Jesus always leading with love? Doesn't he always establish a relationship, show the person he cares, and then help that person see the need to change? And don't we want to follow the example of Jesus?

"You made an assumption about me. Let me make an assumption about you," I continued. "I bet you talk to people

---

*It just so happened I had preached about sin and hell that week. That's not something I do all the time, but I have no fear in doing it, because people know it's coming from a place of love.

about their sin. And I know I talk to people about their sin. The only difference is that when I talk to them about it, they listen to me. And my assumption is that people *don't* listen to you. The reason they listen to me is because I lead with love and establish a relationship first."

Then a bunch of people cheered and some old ladies said, "Amen!" Then the red-faced, big-headed, trucker-hat guy beat the crap out of me. No, not really.

If we are going to help people who are far from God get close to God, we need to tell them the truth, but we *must* lead with God's love.

If our goal is to help people say yes to God's offer and put their faith in Jesus so they can spend eternity in heaven, is scaring them the best we can do? Is God's love so insignificant, is Jesus so unattractive, is heaven so unappealing, that we can't point people there and get them interested? Do we instead have to focus on sin and hell, and hope we can scare people into saying yes to God? And if we scare people into saying yes, is that really love? Jesus said that what's most important is loving God with all we are and with everything we have.[12] If we call people sinners and make them afraid of hell, have we really helped them to love God? And, if we haven't helped them to love God, haven't we failed?

If our goal is to change people's behavior, to get them to repent, is fear really the best way to do that? If every time I left the house my wife said, "If you go meet another woman, I will divorce you," would that be the best motivation for me to be faithful? Or would I eventually come to resent a relationship based on fear? Isn't love a better motivation for faithfulness? Conformity to rules doesn't last. Being coerced into obedience gets tiresome and burdensome. Love is what leads to lasting life change.

But there's a fear Christians have. Back in chapter 1, I promised we'd cover this, so let's address it now. The fear is that if we love sinners without telling them they're sinners, they might take that as an acceptance of sin. They might even view it as license to keep on sinning. I think that concern is what leads many Christians to hold back from really loving people until they stop sinning. We want them to behave first. So instead of leading with love, we lead with truth. We try to change people by telling them truth about their sin. Then if they change and start behaving, we feel like we can offer them love.

And that is the the exact *opposite* of what Jesus did. And, honestly, it's ridiculous.

Shawn Hornbeck disappeared on October 6, 2002, when he was eleven years old. After his disappearance, his mother and stepfather quit their jobs, depleted their savings, and borrowed heavily as they devoted their lives to searching for him. After four years they had nearly given up hope. Then one day the phone rang. The voice on the other end was that of a local prosecutor. He said, "We think we've found Shawn; we're 95 percent sure."

Shawn's stepfather said, "Those were the sweetest words I ever heard in my life." Soon Shawn, by this time fifteen years old, was reunited with his parents.[13]

Now let's imagine that phone call going a bit differently. Let's pretend the prosecutor said, "We think we've found Shawn. We're 95 percent sure. There's only one problem: he was caught shoplifting. It seems that while Shawn was living with his kidnapper, he developed the habit of shoplifting."

How do you think Shawn's parents would have responded? Do you think they'd say, "Well then, we don't want him back"? Or perhaps, "Well, please tell Shawn that he can come back home, but only after he cleans up his act. There will be no shoplifters in our home!"

No way.

I'm sure they would have said, "Shoplifting? Who cares if he was shoplifting? Just bring him home. We need to hold him! We'll talk to him about shoplifting later. In fact, we're confident that once he's back home and experiences our love and provision, he won't feel the need to shoplift anymore. But we're not worried about that right now. We just want him home!"

So why is it okay for us not to judge sin and to instead lead with love?

That's why.

Mistaking grace for an acceptance of sin *is* a mistake, because they are *not* the same. An attitude of accepting sin says, "God loves you just the way you are, so keep doing whatever you're doing." The attitude of grace says, "God loves you just the way you are, but he loves you way too much to leave you that way."[14]

To be honest, the reality is that some *will* mistake grace for an acceptance of sin. But it's worth the risk. How do I know that? Because God is willing to take that risk. God's grace is so amazing and outlandish that people *do* mistake it for an acceptance of sin. That's the way it's *always* been. Check out Romans 6 and you'll see that it was happening two thousand years ago.

If God is willing to offer a grace so amazing, knowing that some would mistake it for acceptance of or license to sin, shouldn't we also be willing to take that risk?

We hope people won't make that mistake, but we offer grace regardless. We speak truth as we go out and proclaim the message, but not like the big-headed guy in the trucker hat probably does, and not like Jonah. We speak the truth but always lead with love.

And not only does leading with love mean we're following the right order, but it also means that rather than offering judgment for their sin, we are immediately offering people the one thing that will meet their deepest and truest need and lead them out of their sin. In his book *Vanishing Grace*, Philip Yancey writes about a day he spent with Henri Nouwen.

He had just returned from San Francisco, where he spent a week in an AIDS clinic visiting patients who, in the days before antiretroviral drugs, faced a certain and agonizing death. "I'm a priest, and as part of my job I listen to people's stories," he told me. "So

I went up and down the ward asking the patients, most of them young men, if they wanted to talk."

Nouwen went on to say that his prayers changed after that week. As he listened to accounts of promiscuity and addiction and self-destructive behavior, he heard hints of a thirst for love that had never been quenched. From then on he prayed, "God, help me to see others not as my enemies or as ungodly but rather as *thirsty* people. And give me the courage and compassion to offer your Living Water, which alone quenches deep thirst."

That day with the gentle priest has stayed with me. Now, whenever I encounter strident skeptics who mock my beliefs or people whose behavior I find offensive, I remind myself of Henri Nouwen's prayer. I ask God to keep me from rushing to judgment or bristling with self-defense. *Let me see them as thirsty people*, I pray, *and teach me how best to present the Living Water.*[15]

The Search for Water

The beginning of the story of Sin City was a search for water. I said earlier that sin always begins with a desperate desert search for water. Check out what God says in Jeremiah 2:13: "My people have committed two sins: They have forsaken me, the spring of living water, and have dug their own cisterns, broken cisterns that cannot hold water."

The idea is that we're all thirsty, metaphorically. We all know there's something more than what we're experiencing, and we long for it. We thirst for it. And God *is it*. Friendship with him, a relationship with him, loving him, worshipping him—that's what we were made for, and it's the *only* thing that will satisfy us, that will quench our thirst.

The problem is that we don't look to God to give us what we're thirsty for, but instead we look elsewhere. This verse says that we dig our own cisterns. So instead of going to God for meaning and joy and satisfaction in life, we look for it and dig for it, in our jobs, in our relationships with people, in success, in sex, in alcohol or drugs. Those things may wet our mouths a little, but they don't quench our thirst. They are "broken cisterns that cannot hold water." When we realize our thirst hasn't been quenched, we go back to the same thing, thinking maybe this time it will satisfy us. *Maybe if I can be a little more successful, make a little more money. Maybe this time when I get drunk . . . maybe this girl I sleep with . . .* So we go down a path of seeking something that only God can give us. But it's a path *away* from God. It's like we're in a desert, desperately searching for water, and it leads to our own sin story.

But God can forgive us. He wants to give us a second chance, and he's calling us back to him. That's why he sent Jesus. Jesus says,

> Let anyone who is thirsty come to me and drink.
> Whoever believes in me, as Scripture has said, rivers
> of living water will flow from within them.[16]

and,

Whoever believes in me will never be thirsty.[17]

and,

Everyone who drinks this water will be thirsty again, but whoever drinks the water I give them will never thirst. Indeed, the water I give them will become in them a spring of water welling up to eternal life.[18]

Are you thirsty? Are you searching for water in the desert? Is it possible you've been searching in the wrong places? You can find the water you need, but only in Jesus. Friendship with him, a relationship with him, loving him and worshiping him is what you were made for, and he's what will satisfy you and quench your thirst.

If you *have* found that living water, are you sharing it with others? We see throughout Jonah's story that he had a compassionless, loveless heart, but at least he told people. God had to tell him twice, but at least he told people.

In the Bible, God has repeatedly told you and me to tell people about him. Not once or twice—*repeatedly*.

If we refuse to tell people about Jesus, if we're not sharing God's message of grace, *we are Jonah*.

11

GOD FOR THE PIMP

WHEN YOU WERE A KID, people may have described you using words like "cute" or "talkative" or "adorable" or "obsessed with toys."

Growing up, Travis was "entrepreneurial" and "independent" and "a hustler" and "obsessed with money." He was always that way. He says he learned early on that if you ask enough people to buy something, eventually someone's going to buy it. He was always trying to sell someone something, always trying to manipulate a situation or a person to his advantage, always trying to get more bank.

By the age of twenty-five, Travis had a wife and a kid, and was making good money, but he didn't see a path to making

GOD FOR THE REST OF US

more. One day he asked his dad, "Where's all the money in America?" His father replied, "Las Vegas." That was all Travis needed to hear.

He had never been to Vegas, never even been out of New York City, but he put his wife and kid in a car and left. He had no plan for how he'd get all the money in Las Vegas into his pocket, but he'd think of something. He'd hustle. He'd ask a bunch of people to buy something, and eventually someone would buy it.

When Travis got to Vegas, he immediately gravitated to Sin City's nightclubs and strip clubs. Travis had a background in photography and quickly saw his play. He started asking the managers of the clubs, "How about you make me your photographer?"

They laughed and said, "We don't need a photographer."

"Sure you do," he told them, and pretty quickly Travis was the photographer for ten clubs and was employing twelve photographers, who would take pictures of the partyers, sell the pictures as mementos,* and feature them on the night-clubs' websites.

Travis was making good money again, and working in the nightclub industry meant he was partying and drinking for free. His dreams had come true, but it still wasn't enough.

Soon he was recruiting girls to work in the strip clubs. And he started asking the strippers, "How about you make me your photographer?"

---

*Probably for many, that photo would be the only memory they had of the night.

They'd give him a weird look and say, "But I don't need a photographer."

"Sure you do," he'd explain, and soon he was photographing Vegas's strippers.

Then Travis was sleeping with Vegas's strippers.

Since moving to Vegas, Travis's wife had given birth to their second child. When she found out her husband was sleeping around, she walked out with the kids. Travis didn't care. He had other girls now. He could spend the night with just about anyone he wanted.

And yet it still wasn't enough.

So Travis started hustling the girls. He'd tell them his story and where he was going. And he'd say, "You want to go where I'm going?"

The girls would smile and ask, "For real?"

"Yeah," Travis would tell them. "Only one thing. If we're going to get where we're going, we're going to need some money. You know how to get some money?"

Travis showed the girls how they could make more money with their bodies than they could by just dancing in a strip club. And Travis began managing them. Some girls were making him a thousand dollars a night.

Travis's hustle was to make the girls fall in love with him. Then he could get them to do whatever he wanted. He called it his "mind play." And when the occasional girl got fed up with him or tired of living that life, it didn't really matter, because there was always another girl out there.

One morning when Travis woke up, he looked next to

him in bed and saw one of the girls lying there. He walked into the bathroom and looked at himself in the mirror.

Travis had everything he'd ever wanted. He was living the dream.[1]

The Question

So here's a question I had to wrestle with: Is God for Travis? Is he for a pimp who sleeps with girls and sells them for money? Is he for this guy who betrayed his wife and left his kids without a father?

Jesus showed us that God is for the prostitute. But there's something different about Travis's situation. When the prostitute came bursting into the Pharisee's dinner party, she was already repentant. She had engaged in vulgar sins, but she had decided to turn away from that life. So we might conclude that this was the reason Jesus was for her. It makes sense that God would be for her once she'd made that decision. But Travis was still living it up in the destructive tragedy of his sin.

Before we answer this question, let's meet another woman who met Jesus. One who, like Travis, was still living it up in the destructive tragedy of her sin.

Caught in the Act

Like Travis, this woman was in bed with someone to whom she was not married.

Unlike Travis, the eyes staring back at her were not her own. They were the flinty eyes of the Pharisees and the teachers of the law. These men were well known. She had seen them many times around town, giving disapproving stares to anyone they considered beneath them, which was everyone. The problem is that this time they weren't around town; they were in her bedroom. Their disapproving stares were for her. And she was not only beneath them; she was in bed beneath a man who was not her husband.

As they grabbed her and pulled her out of the room, she screamed in fear. She tried to reach for her clothes, for a bedsheet, for anything to cover her nakedness.

Suddenly she was being marched across town for all to see in a parade of shame, her confusion and humiliation increasing with each step.

She realized they were taking her to the Temple. A torrent of thoughts must have flooded her mind: *Why are they taking me to the Temple? Are they going to take me inside? Will they kill me? In the Temple?*

But then they stopped, just outside it, in the Temple courts. She heard one of the men speak: "Teacher, this woman was caught in the act of adultery. In the Law Moses commanded us to stone such women. Now what do you say?"[2]

The woman frantically surveyed the scene. Through tear-filled eyes, she could see the men beginning to encircle her, stones in hand, and she realized their intention *was* to kill her.

And then she saw *him*.

There was a man crouching on the ground. A crowd was gathered around him. The man was writing on the ground, in the dirt, with his finger. He seemed to be ignoring them. He wouldn't answer their question. What did that mean for her? Did they need his permission to kill her?

The Pharisees, who would not loosen their grip on her now-throbbing arms, continued to question the man, demanding an answer.

Finally he looked up and said, "Let any one of you who is without sin be the first to throw a stone at her."[3]

That's it, she thought, *my death sentence.* These men were known for being sinless. She held her breath and waited for the first stone to strike her.

But instead it struck the ground.

One of the Pharisees had dropped his stone.

Then another.

And another.

And another.

And another.

And the hands that had been holding her so firmly released their grip.

The men all walked away.[4]

She was dazed. She didn't know what to do. So she just stood there. She stood there and did the math in her head. Apparently, only someone without sin could judge someone else for his or her sin. And since it turned out that everyone there actually *had* sinned, there was no one who could judge or punish her for her wrongdoing.

Finally, the man stood up and asked, "Woman, where are they? Has no one condemned you?"[5]

She had just been caught in the act of adultery. She was standing naked in front of this man who apparently had some kind of authority over even the religious leaders. And he was speaking to her.

"No one, sir," she said.[6]

She still wasn't sure what was happening, but she saw something in his eyes: compassion.

"Then neither do I condemn you," Jesus declared. "Go now and leave your life of sin."[7]

Without Sin

There was an Old Testament law. The law said that someone guilty of adultery was to be stoned to death.

We learn in this story that, according to Jesus, the only person fit to condemn and punish someone for breaking the law is someone without sin.

That makes sense.*

I mean, we don't actually live that way. We condemn people all the time for their sins, despite being guilty of plenty of our own.

We judge the girl who strips off her clothes in the club, despite the fact that we strip people of their dignity when we talk down to them like they're less important than we are.

---

*Not only does it make sense that sinners can't judge other sinners, but we are specifically prohibited, in 1 Corinthians 5:12-13, from judging non-Christians. Ironically, non-Christians are almost always the people who Christians *do* judge. We judge them for not living up to God's standards, standards they have never agreed to live up to. And we judge them despite the fact that we are told *not* to in the Bible. So when a Christian judges a non-Christian, the Christian is sinning.

We condemn the guy who lusts over pornography, despite the fact that we lust after money and popularity.

We disapprove of the unmarried couple living together, despite the fact that we live in marriages that don't honor God because we don't love one other as Jesus loved the church.

We denounce the girl wearing the low-cut shirt that reveals too much of her body, despite the fact that we gossip and reveal secrets we promised to keep.

We castigate the smoker inhaling nicotine during his work break, despite the fact that we'll inhale three donuts during our work break.

We vilify the man dealing drugs on the street corner, despite the fact that we deal half-truths in business transactions.

I'm not saying that stripping or looking at pornography or living together isn't wrong. It is. It's rebellion against and violates the nature of a holy God. It damages the lives of others. If we do those things, they demean us and lead us to live "less-than" lives. I'm not saying any of it is okay. I'm just saying that we're not in a place to cast stones. Well, actually, *I'm* not saying that. *Jesus* did.

We tend to judge the sin of others. But when we read the story of the woman caught in adultery and hear Jesus' words, it makes sense that only someone without sin can judge someone else's sin. Just like only someone without sin can take the punishment for someone else's sin.

All the Pharisees and teachers of the law, despite the righteous facade they lived behind, *had* sinned. So they couldn't judge the sin of someone else.

GOD FOR THE PIMP

But there *was* someone there that day without sin: Jesus. So Jesus *was* in a position to judge her. In fact, the situation called for Jesus to uphold the law and enforce the punishment it demanded.

But no, Jesus said, "Neither do I condemn you."

Maybe that bothers you. Perhaps it doesn't, but it should. It might not bother us because our hearts go out to victims, and it's easy to feel like this woman was a victim. In one sense, she was. The Pharisees were using her, and she was suffering public humiliation. But she was certainly not *just* a victim. She had made the choice to commit adultery. She was cheating on her husband, or breaking up the marriage of another woman, or both. She had sinned. Just minutes earlier she was found in the middle of committing the sin. She didn't come forward. She didn't confess it. She was *caught*. And we have absolutely no indication that she, at any time, believed in Jesus. She didn't even know who he was, calling him "sir." She wasn't coming to faith. She wasn't repentant. If she'd had her way, she would probably have *still* been living it up in the destructive tragedy of her sin.

So why didn't Jesus condemn her? He was without sin. He was in a position to do so. And it was what the law required. Her sin had to be punished.

Honestly, I'm not sure I know the answer. We know Jesus wasn't one to ignore the law or to ignore sin, but it is very obvious that Jesus was for this guilty, unrepentant, no-faith sinner.

One thing that seems clear to me from this story is that we

are not defined by our sins. That's what the men wanted to do with this woman. To them, she was an adulterer. She was a sinner caught in her sin. But that's not how Jesus viewed her. She was some father's daughter. She had a mother who had dreamed about who her daughter might become. Most important, she was a child of God. And despite her sin, she was still loved by him.

What we seem to learn from this story is that while we certainly need to take our sins seriously, our sins don't define us. We're not worthless because of our sins. And for that matter, we're also not worthwhile because of the good we've done. Our worth is based on God's love for us. The Bible says in 1 John 3:1, "See what great love the Father has lavished on us, that we should be called children of God! And that is what we are!" We are not defined by our sin but by God's love.

By now some people reading this book might be wondering if I am "soft on sin." But the person we should really be wondering about is Jesus. I mean, sure, as the woman began to walk away, having completely gotten away with her wrongdoing, Jesus did call out, "Don't keep on sinning," but come on, that wasn't even a slap on the wrist. It was just some good advice. Jesus didn't follow the law and stone her. He didn't punish her in any way. He didn't even give her a stern talking to.

So was Jesus soft on sin?

Well, not long after that woman was forced to stand before him, Jesus went to the cross.

Why?

Because her sin *had to be punished.* The character of a holy and just God requires it. The law demanded it. Her sin debt had to be paid.

So Jesus did it himself.

Jesus used his sinlessness not as a position to judge and condemn her sin but to position himself on the cross, where he could take the judgment and condemnation she deserved.

"You see, at just the right time, when we were still powerless, Christ died for the ungodly. Very rarely will anyone die for a righteous person, though for a good person someone might possibly dare to die. But God demonstrates his own love for us in this: While we were still sinners, Christ died for us."[8]

Jesus died for us, and for the woman caught in adultery, when we were at our worst.

And God was for her, even when she was still a guilty, unrepentant, no-faith sinner.

I Didn't Know I Could Be Loved Like That

Travis woke up that day, his wallet, as always, stuffed with cash. A girl other guys would pay for was lying in the bed next to him. He walked into the bathroom and looked at himself in the mirror.

Travis had everything he ever wanted. He was living the dream.

And he felt sick.

He realized he had it all, but for some reason it still felt like he had nothing.

He looked at himself, thinking, *This is not the dream. Something has to change. I'm going to kill myself or something.* Then a surprising thought hit him. *I want my family back.*

He contacted his wife. She was dubious. She told him she had started going to church with the kids. Travis asked if he could join them. He had never been to church. Growing up, he had heard his parents speak of religion only in a negative way. He had no interest in church, but if that was the only way to get his family back . . .

That Sunday my message just happened to be on Luke 15.

As Travis listened to the story of the Prodigal Son who had squandered the treasure he had been given on "wild living," he realized that was exactly what he had done in Las Vegas. He had squandered his life on wild living. Eventually the son had nothing. Travis thought, *I have nothing. I have a graveyard inside of me.*

Travis held his breath as the son made his journey home, and he was overcome when he learned that the son was still welcomed home, that the father was happy to have his son back. He was amazed that the father didn't even correct him. But then he understood: the wild living had taken its toll on that young man. So the father didn't have to correct him. And Travis knew that story was about him. *After all the partying, after all the destruction I have caused in my family's life, God doesn't have to correct me. He will just take me back.*

In that moment, Travis felt the most indescribable love.

He listened to me conclude the message: "It doesn't matter who you are; God still loves you. It doesn't matter why you left; God is still pursuing you, just like the shepherd pursued the one lost sheep. It doesn't matter where you've been or what you've done; God will still take you back, just like the father took back the Prodigal Son." Travis started weeping. Uncontrollably. Inconsolably.

A few minutes later, just after the service ended, I met Travis for the first time. He walked up to me and tried to speak, but I couldn't understand a word he was saying. He was broken up. Finally, he calmed himself down enough to say, "I didn't know I could be loved like that."

But What Happens Next?

The part that bothers me most about the story from John 8 is that we don't know what happened to the woman. Jesus told her to go and sin no more. Did she obey him? Or did she go back to the man and her old way of life? We don't know. But I have a guess. In fact, I'd bet on it.* My guess is that the grace Jesus showed her turned her life around. I feel confident that experiencing the compassion of Jesus made her submit to his authority. That's the impact God's grace tends to have on a person. Rules generally push people away and lead them to rebelliousness. Love generally pulls people close and leads them to faithfulness.

---

*Sorry. Living in Vegas, we're required to say things like "I'd bet on it" and "I want to hit the jackpot!" and, before putting our money in the offering plate at church, "What kind of odds am I getting?"

That's definitely what happened with Travis.

I gave Travis a couple days to stop crying, and then we met at a coffee shop.

He now knew God loved him, but he knew nothing about this God who loved him. He had a million questions.* Was this all true? What did it mean for his life? What were his next steps?

I tried to answer them all, and we met again and again.

Travis became the first person we ever baptized at our then–baby church. We did it in the hot tub behind the casino we were meeting in at the time.** "Looking back at the person who went into the water," Travis says of that day, "that person was dead. The picture of baptism is just beautiful. You go down and you're buried in this grave, and then you're resurrected. And looking back, I'm a completely different person. It's wild."

And he's right. He is a completely different person. That first day in church, Travis's heart was assaulted by God's love, and now it bleeds gratitude. He experienced a grace explosion in the depths of his being, and he hasn't been the same since.

At our church we have invite cards available for people to give to their friends. It's not unusual for a person to take a couple. What *is* unusual is for a person to take a couple hundred, but that's exactly what Travis started doing. He was giving cards to everyone, everywhere he went. He just wanted

---

*Not literally. Literally, he had closer to thirty-five questions.
**Which is, most assuredly, the *only* holy thing that has ever happened in that hot tub.

everyone to know this God he was getting to know, and he wanted them to experience the love that had changed his life.

Travis had some background in hip-hop music, so he started writing and recording songs about God and giving them out as free CDs.

He started hanging out with homeless people so he could tell them about Jesus. He learned that homeless people in Las Vegas desperately need socks. So he went to dozens of churches asking if they'd help him collect new socks to give out. He then threw a block party in a poor urban area, giving countless pairs of socks to the homeless.

One day Travis realized that college is where kids tend to make important decisions about their lives, so he started hanging out at UNLV, made friends there, and was soon leading a Bible study full of students.

Travis thought about the people he had become friends with in his former life and started going back to visit them. Soon he was doing a one-on-one weekly Bible study with one of the major pimps in Las Vegas.

The growing, trendy, artsy area in Las Vegas right now is around Fremont Street, and every time I talk to Travis lately, he's asking me to help him figure out how he can let the people there know that God is for them. In fact, he just started a band so he can play in bars on Fremont Street and share Jesus with the people there.

Travis says, "I don't necessarily try to explain what happened to me, 'cause it's something that's unexplainable. And that's what miracles are. The biggest testimony I have is that my life changed. This is who I was then, and this is who I am now. And something happened in the middle that transformed me. There's only one word I can think of, and it's 'love.' We misuse that word all the time. I 'love' this and I 'love' that. But we don't know what love is until we meet Jesus."

That's it.

Travis taught me that God's love is even for the guilty. It's for a woman caught in the act of adultery. And for an adulterous pimp who wakes up every morning with a different one of his girls in bed with him. God doesn't give up on them. He continues to reach out to them and eventually transforms them.

And his love will change *your* life, if you just let it.

His love will change the lives of everyone you know, if you just share it with them.

12

GOD FOR THOSE WHO HAVE BEEN TURNED OFF BY CHURCH

Do you remember the movie from 1994 called *The Mask*? For a few months it had you and everyone you know saying, "Sssssssssmokin'!"

Adapted from a comic-book series and starring Jim Carrey, the movie centers on Stanley Ipkiss, a guy who finds a magical mask that depicts Loki, the Norse god of darkness and mischief.*

Stanley puts on the mask, and it turns out that when he wears it, not only does it hide his true self, but it also allows him to become something different. It allows him to project a different persona.

---

*Fortunately he didn't find the mask of Richard Simmons, the fitness guru of the 1980s who was famous for his candy-striped shorts and bedazzled tank tops.

At first, Stanley can choose when he wants to wear the mask. He uses it as a way to escape from and transform reality. But over time, the mask takes over. Stanley becomes increasingly dependent on it. In fact, the mask starts to control his life.

It seems that this illustration is true for so many people. It's easier to let our masks—what we hide behind or the false self we project to others—take over our lives.

We have a name for that. We call a person who lives behind a mask a hypocrite—a person who shows you one thing when the reality is something else is a hypocrite.

For some reason, a lot of Christians seem to be especially skilled at this. It's what turns so many people away from the church.

The Man behind the Pastor Mask

One day when we were in the process of starting Verve, I received a phone call. I was walking out of the warehouse we were renovating to serve as our church building. I was feeling the stress of the financial burden of planting a new church. The phone ringing was an annoying interruption to my agenda. I didn't recognize the number, but I took the call.

The person calling identified himself as a pastor who had read my books and heard me speak and was excited for what we were doing in Las Vegas. He wanted to help. His church took an annual Christmas Eve offering, which they would give away to another ministry or church. This year they wanted to give the offering to Verve. I was grateful, but I assumed it would be a small offering.

Then he said, "We don't know for sure how much people will give, but we know it would help your planning to have some idea, so we'll guarantee that we'll give you at least $25,000."

Sssssssmokin'!

I thought, *Wow, that's not what I was expecting!*

So I thanked him profusely and hung up, thinking, *Who is this guy?*

I did some research. I learned he was a relatively young but very respected up-and-coming pastor of a new but rapidly growing church. He came from a very impressive family.

Three years later I learned that he was actually having an affair with a woman on his staff, *and* drinking a bottle or two of whiskey every night, *and* abusing drugs, *and* physically abusing his wife.

One night he grabbed two of his guns, made some threatening comments, and left the house. His wife had a restraining order put on him, to keep him away from her and the kids.

As she went through his stuff, she found a suicide note he had written months earlier—though he had not gone through with the suicide—in which he said, "I have become what I never wished to be."

In the suicide note he gave exact directions for how he wanted his funeral to be, and he even provided his own obituary. In real life he is five feet eight inches tall. However, in the obituary he wrote for himself, he listed his height at five feet eleven and three-quarters inches tall. The mask had so taken over his life that he couldn't even be honest about the obvious. And I learned all that and thought, *Who is this guy?*

Apparently, he was a guy who, at some point in his life, found a mask. He put it on, and it allowed him to live two lives. He was a loving, respected pastor, *and* he was a drug-using, alcoholic, abusive husband who cheated on his wife.

He was a hypocrite.

And my guess is that a lot of people will turn away from church because of his example.

Unfortunately, situations like this one are not that unusual. Tens of thousands, maybe hundreds of thousands of people have been turned off by church. There are many reasons, but probably one of the most common is hypocrisy.

When surveys ask people the reasons why they don't go to church, hypocrisy is right at the top of the list. It may be the hypocrisy of a famous televangelist or pastor or churchgoing coworker or neighbor.

You might be one of those people who stopped going to church because you've been turned off by religious hypocrites. If you are, it may help you to know that Jesus was turned off by religious hypocrites as well.

Jesus and the Hypocrites

In Jesus' day, there was a group of religious leaders called the Pharisees. They were respected and revered by everyone for the holy lives they lived out for all to see.

But what they showed people was not the truth. Jesus was

able to see beyond the pretense, beyond the facade. And what he saw on the inside of these religious leaders did not match up with what they showed the world on the outside.

Jesus had repeated confrontations with the Pharisees. One of the most heated is recorded for us in Matthew 23: "Then Jesus said to the crowds and to his disciples: 'The teachers of the law and the Pharisees sit in Moses' seat. So you must be careful to do everything they tell you. But do not do what they do, for they do not practice what they preach. They tie up heavy, cumbersome loads and put them on other people's shoulders, but they themselves are not willing to lift a finger to move them. Everything they do is done for people to see.'"[1]

Jesus, in front of the Pharisees, speaks to the crowds *about* the Pharisees. The Pharisees spend most of their time preaching, "Do what we're telling you." Jesus says, "Do what they tell you, but don't follow their example. They do it all for show."

Then he turns and faces the Pharisees and speaks directly to them. "Woe to you, teachers of the law and Pharisees, you hypocrites! You shut the door of the kingdom of heaven in people's faces. You yourselves do not enter, nor will you let those enter who are trying to. Woe to you, teachers of the law and Pharisees, you hypocrites! You travel over land and sea to win a single convert, and when you have succeeded, you make them twice as much a child of hell as you are."[2]

Yowza. Jesus, why don't you tell us how you *really* feel?

He does. He continues with, "Woe to you, teachers of the law and Pharisees, you hypocrites! You give a tenth of your spices—mint, dill and cumin. But you have neglected the more important matters of the law—justice, mercy and faithfulness. You should have practiced the latter, without neglecting the former. You blind guides! You strain out a gnat but swallow a camel. Woe to you, teachers of the law and Pharisees, you hypocrites! You clean the outside of the cup and dish, but inside they are full of greed and self-indulgence. Blind Pharisee! First clean the inside of the cup and dish, and then the outside also will be clean. Woe to you, teachers of the law and Pharisees, you hypocrites! You are like whitewashed tombs, which look beautiful on the outside but on the inside are full of the bones of the dead and everything unclean. In the same way, on the outside you appear to people as righteous but on the inside you are full of hypocrisy and wickedness."[3]

Jesus repeatedly calls the Pharisees "hypocrites." Back then the word *hypocrite* referred to actors who performed onstage. The actors would wear masks because often the same actor would play several different parts. He might wear a mask that made him look like a rich man in one scene, then change to a mask depicting a poor woman in another. The masks were large, with exaggerated facial features and expressions so people in the back of the audience could see them. Inside the mask was a megaphone-type device allowing the actor to project his voice to the very back row. These masks were called *prosopa*, which later became *persona*.

Jesus is quoted as using the word *hypocrite* eighteen times in the Bible, and every time, he uses it to describe a person who wears a mask, not on a stage, but in life—someone who projects an image that doesn't reflect that person's true reality. These people, like the Pharisees, create personas. They wear masks that allow them to be someone else.

Jesus' critique of hypocrites isn't so much that people aren't what they should be on the inside. The problem is that they're giving the impression they're something they're not, on the outside. The issue isn't really the interior brokenness, selfishness, and sinfulness as much as it is the false exterior displayed to others. It's *deception* that makes a person a hypocrite.

How Should We Respond to Hypocrisy?

Hypocrisy is a problem. So what do we do about it?

Perhaps you're kind of on the outside—outside the church, outside Christianity—looking in with disdain at the hypocrites. You need to understand that even though hypocrisy has kept you away from Jesus, Jesus actually has the same disdain for hypocrisy that you have. So it really doesn't make sense for hypocrisy to keep you from Jesus, even if it is the hypocrisy of people who claim to be his followers. The way hypocrisy repels you makes it even more obvious how attracted you would be to Jesus if you really got to know him, because he was the most unhypocritical person and taught the most unhypocritical way of life ever.

Could it be that you've been rejecting the wrong thing?

Think of it this way: let's say you go to a restaurant and have a *Kitchen Nightmares* kind of experience.* The

---

*If you've never seen *Kitchen Nightmares*, you should be imagining one of America's worst restaurants and a British guy yelling obscenities at the owners.

ambiance is dreary, the service is awful, the food is cold and bland, and no one apologizes. You would judge that restaurant. And you should. But you wouldn't judge *all* restaurants based on that *one* experience. And you wouldn't stop eating food. You would understand that food isn't to blame for the bad service you received. Right? That's just logical.

But for some reason we don't apply that same logic to church. If a person who claims he's a Christian is a hypocrite or if a pastor is a hypocrite, it makes sense to judge *that* Christian or *that* pastor. But it doesn't make sense to judge *all* Christians based on that one experience.

If a *church* practiced hypocrisy, it would make sense for you to no longer want to attend *that* church, but not to give up on all churches altogether.

And it definitely doesn't make sense to stop seeking Jesus. Jesus isn't to blame for the bad experience you had with one Christian or with one church. In fact, he's as upset about it as you are.

Some people who call themselves Christians *are* hypocrites. But that's not every Christian. There *are* some churches that are led by and filled with hypocrites. But that's not every church. I actually think these situations are kind of rare. It's just that they're really noticeable and unforgettable when you see them.

I would challenge you to evaluate each person and each church individually. It's not fair to judge them all together. It's not fair to them, and (more important) *it's not fair to you.* Because if you lump them all together, call them all hypocrites, and reject all of Christianity, it could keep you from Jesus. And that's not fair to you, because Jesus is what you need.

But I need to offer a word of caution. You may want to be careful when you judge, because, honestly, you're probably at least a little bit of a hypocrite yourself.

That last sentence may have made you angry, but be honest: Do you perfectly live out what you believe?

Maybe there are some things about healthy eating or exercising that you believe but don't always practice.

Perhaps you have some beliefs about marriage or parenting that you don't always practice.

It could even be that you have beliefs about God and faith that you don't always practice.

And I'm guessing you sometimes project to other people something better than your reality. Maybe it's a first date and you're out to impress. Or you're the lady whose online dating profile has a picture of you from ten years ago when you were twenty pounds lighter. Or you're the guy whose says you enjoy romantic movies and long walks in the moonlight, instead of the truth: you enjoy watching football and eating chicken wings . . . in your underwear.

Or perhaps at work you have this facade you live behind because you think it's your path to success.

Or maybe you have some deep, dark secrets you don't let anyone know because that's not what you want people to think about you.

I think the truth is that we all wear masks. And if you were really honest, you might admit that you're a bit of a hypocrite yourself.

But that's hard to admit. I had one of those moments recently, and it had to do with the pastor whose congregation gave our church $25,000. I had just learned of his true character, of what was going on with him behind closed doors. I got on the Internet and read some articles that exposed his secret sins.

I couldn't believe it. I talked with my wife about it. I criticized him: "How could he walk up on stage each week representing God, teaching people from the Bible, when he was living that kind of life? How dare he treat his wife that way? What kind of idiot writes his own obituary and lies about his height in it?"

One night I was lying in bed, and I realized I had spent far more time criticizing him than praying for him. Do you know what that makes me? A hypocrite.

Because I say I'm living a life of love. And I believe in the power of prayer. And I know that God can change people. Even people who have messed up their lives can have a second chance with God. With God, there's no such thing as too far or too late.

And even still my thoughts were dominated by criticism for that man's past instead of prayer for his future.

I'm a hypocrite.

Do you know what that makes me feel? Disdain for myself.

So you may want to be careful when you judge, because you may be a bit of a hypocrite yourself.

What if you realize that's true? What if you realize you're a hypocrite? Maybe you're not on the outside looking in; you might be on the inside—inside church, inside Christianity—looking at yourself, and you have some disdain for yourself. Perhaps, because you live life behind a mask, you realize you're part of the problem.

What do you do?

You go to Jesus.

Because Jesus cleans people from the inside out. Not only is he for those who are turned off by hypocrisy, he's for hypocrites. He hates hypocrisy, but he is for hypocrites.

The amazing thing is that no matter what your problem is, even something as objectionable as hypocrisy, Jesus still loves you. He loves you as you are, not as you should be.

And he's able to help you out of your hypocrisy. He's able to transform a hypocrite who doesn't want to be a hypocrite anymore.

One time a Pharisee named Nicodemus came to Jesus in the middle of the night: "'Rabbi, we know that you are a teacher who has come from God. For no one could perform the signs you are doing if God were not with him.' Jesus replied, 'Very truly I tell you, no one can see the kingdom of God unless they are born again.'"[4]

Nicodemus came in the middle of the night because he was afraid. He was afraid because he wore a mask that told people he was the one who had all the answers about God. So what would people think if they knew Nicodemus was going to Jesus, asking him questions about God?

Jesus explained to Nicodemus that for him to become a part of the kingdom of God, for him to be right with God, he would have to be "born again." Basically, Jesus was telling Nicodemus that he'd have to start all over because he had it all wrong. Nicodemus thought it was about the outside—what people can see. But it's about the inside—what only God can see. In effect, he was telling Nicodemus, "You're fixated on the outside, but what you need to fix is on the inside."

They went on to have a fascinating conversation in which Jesus talked about choosing to live in the light rather than the darkness, and in which Jesus said, "God so loved the world that he gave his one and only Son, that whoever believes in him shall not perish but have eternal life. For God did not send his Son into the world to condemn the world, but to save the world through him."[5]

I think Jesus was letting Nicodemus know that despite Nicodemus's hypocrisy, he was still loved by God. And that Jesus' purpose was not to condemn him but to save him from his sins, including his sin of hypocrisy.

Eighteen hundred years later Søren Kierkegaard wrote, "There comes a midnight hour when everyone must unmask." I think that's what Jesus hoped would happen with Nicodemus that night.

I imagine that conversation left Nicodemus deep in difficult thought. He was probably wondering, *Am I willing to walk away from what I've believed, from how I've lived, so I can have this Jesus who—despite what's behind the mask, despite my secrets, despite the ugliness inside me—loves me and came for me, not to condemn me for my sins but to save me from them, and to offer me eternal life?*

Perhaps you need to wrestle with the same question. Are you willing to walk away from what you've believed (maybe that all Christians are hypocrites and that you would never be one), and from how you've lived (maybe like you don't need God and you don't need faith in anything but yourself), so you can have Jesus who—*despite what's behind the mask, despite your secrets, despite the ugliness inside you*—loves you and came for you, not to condemn you for your sins, but to save you from them and to offer you eternal life?

Eventually Nicodemus decided the answer for him was yes. We see this later in the Bible when Jesus was crucified.

Three days later, Jesus would rise from the dead, and people would put their faith in him again.

But at this point he was hanging dead on a cross.

Everyone had deserted him earlier, but there were two people who risked their lives by showing their allegiance to Jesus. They went to the authorities and asked if they could take Jesus' body down and give him a proper burial. The authorities said yes, and these two men (in front of everyone) took Jesus' body to a grave.

One of these two men was Nicodemus.[6]

And he did it in broad daylight, for everyone to see, even his fellow Pharisees. He didn't care, because he had made a decision in his heart to put his faith in Jesus and to live life unmasked; he decided that from then on, his outside would match his inside.

How about you? Have you made that decision?

If you're on the inside of the church and Christianity and you realize you're a bit of a hypocrite, remember that Jesus *does* condemn hypocrisy. But he didn't come to condemn *you*, he came to *save* you, and he can save you from your hypocrisy. The beautiful truth I've learned is that God is not just for those who have been turned off by the church. He's even for the hypocrites who turned them off.

If you're on the outside of the church and Christianity, and you've had disdain for the hypocrites inside the church, I apologize, because at times I'm part of the problem. But it's time to come back to Jesus and to his church, to join a community of his followers who are committed to living life without masks.

And, honestly, that's what you want, isn't it—to be known and loved for who you really are?

13

GOD FOR THE FORGOTTEN

Gary was six years old when his father walked out and started a new family. After that, Gary's few memories of his dad are of the disappointment of unkept promises. Gary's dad would promise to send a card, to call, to visit. He almost never did.

Gary was left with a mother who never said, "I love you." He felt unwanted. That feeling was confirmed when his mother was on her deathbed and spoke her last words, telling Gary she hated him and wished he had never been born.

Gary turned to alcohol, drugs, and girls. He had friends to party with, as long as he was paying. Countless times Gary woke up lying next to a Dumpster in an alley behind a bar. Where were the friends he had been with the night before?

One night, Gary overdosed and had a minor heart attack while he was at a concert with some friends. He went to the hospital alone. Not one person visited.

I once sent Gary an e-mail asking, "Have you ever felt like a forgotten person?" Gary's response: "The question should be, was there ever a time I *didn't* feel forgotten?"

Despite all this, Gary did well in his career, rising to management positions in a number of posh New York City hotels. Yet repeatedly, Gary's bosses used his ideas without giving him credit and had him do extra work without any recognition. Forgotten again.

Perhaps worst of all, Gary felt forgotten by himself. All the dreams he had ever harbored were gone, and he became lost. He wondered whether it would matter if he ceased to exist. Would anyone miss him? He tried to lose himself, day after day, in drugs and alcohol.

Gary wasn't sure if there was a God. But as he looked back on all the trauma of his life, there were only two logical conclusions: either there was no God, or there was a God who was ignoring him.

Gary felt alone. It was him against the world. In fact, he adopted a personal motto: D.T.A.

"Don't trust anyone!"

You

Perhaps Gary's story resonates with you.

Maybe you never felt loved by your mother.

Or you sit alone every day at lunch.

Your husband walked out on you. Or you're still married, but you feel like your spouse has become a stranger.

You're a teenager who retreats to your bedroom every day after school, seldom coming out.

Or your spouse passed away years ago, and your kids rarely call or visit. The only voices you hear on a typical day come from your television.

You know the pain of feeling forgotten.

Hagar

Hagar was from Egypt. She had probably grown up poor, with no real hope for a better future. Without aspirations, she likely was pleased with the job she had landed, working as a maid for a woman named Sarai.

Sarai's husband was a man named Abram.* He was in his eighties and was a believer in what Hagar considered a foreign god. In fact, the weird thing about Abram was that he believed there was only *one* God. In Egypt, her people believed in a pantheon of gods, but for Abram there was only one. And Abram claimed that this one true God had spoken to him and promised to give him children.

That alleged promise was made years ago, but still Sarai was childless. In Abram and Sarai's culture, there was little worse than being a barren woman, so Hagar understood why Sarai seemed so bitter, so desperate.

One day Sarai went to Abram and asked him to sleep with

*Abram would later be called Abraham.

Hagar. This was a somewhat common practice back then. The legal system even spelled out how such procedures were to go. If the servant gave birth to a child, it belonged to the father and his wife, not to the servant, even though she was the mother.

So Sarai went to Abram and said, "The Lord has kept me from having children. Go, sleep with my maidservant; perhaps I can build a family through her."[1]

The next sentence is classic. It's utterly sad, and pretty funny, all at the same time.

"Abram agreed to what Sarai said."[2]

Abram was like, "Ok, fine, twist my arm. I'll sleep with her, but only because you insist."

They slept together. Hagar got pregnant. And Hagar began to resent Sarai. Perhaps she felt used. She had reason to; she *had* been used. She was probably angry, knowing that the baby would not be seen as her own.

Sarai offered no compassion; instead, she became furious with Hagar. She went to Abram in a rage.

This was Abram's chance to step into the situation, to help Sarai empathize with Hagar's plight, to bring reconciliation to the relationship. Abram did none of that. He told Sarai to do whatever she wanted with Hagar.

Can you imagine how that made Hagar feel? They had shared a night of intimacy. She was carrying his baby. Soon she would give birth to his child. Yet he wouldn't defend her even for a second. Instead, Abram gave Sarai permission to abuse Hagar.

And that's exactly what she did. Sarai began to mistreat and abuse Hagar.

How did that make Hagar feel?

My guess?

Forgotten.

Gary Runs

Gary eventually married, but he never trusted his wife. A lifetime of pain had left him unable to offer love to her and receive love from her in return. The marriage was hollow.

Gary had one thing going for him, though: his job. Until 9/11. The aftermath of the terrorist attack left New York City reeling, forced tourists to stay away, and led many empty hotels to lay off employees. And Gary was one of the employees left without a job.

So Gary ran to Las Vegas.

Why Las Vegas? I don't know, but I do know it's incredibly common. Ask people in any city why they moved there, and you will hear, over and over, "I got a job here" or "I moved here to be closer to my family and friends." Ask people in Las Vegas why they moved here, and you will hear, over and over, "I was running from something" or "I had to start my life over, and Las Vegas seemed like the place to do it."

So Gary took his wife and ran to Las Vegas, where he was able to use his hotel-management experience to get a job in one of Sin City's hotel-casinos. Gary worked his way up to pitboss, but he didn't enjoy his job. He realized that his job was basically to bring misery to people by taking their money. That only added to his misery. And as Gary spent more and more time in the casino, he added gambling to his list of addictions.

Where Do You Run?

Where do you run when you feel forgotten?

Perhaps your deep-soul loneliness has led you to move to a new city every two or three years, or to hold a string of jobs. With each change, you hope that different will be better, but it always ends up the same. Why? You can't run from yourself.

Or when you feel alone, do you run to an addiction? Drugs, alcohol, gambling, pornography, cheesecake?* For a fleeting moment, your endorphins kick in, and you feel something. The problem is, giving in to your addiction always leaves you feeling worse.

Maybe you run to the arms of another man.

Or you run to a novel, video game, or movie so you can fantasize about having a life that isn't your own.

Or you run to your bedroom to get away from your family.

Or you run to your volunteer work, not because of love or because it's the right thing to do, but because it allows you to get away from the isolated life you're trying to escape.

Forgotten people run.

---

*I prefer ice cream. About half a gallon. Chocolate with mint or peanut butter, please.

Hagar Ran

And run is exactly what Hagar did.

She felt mistreated, abandoned, rejected, and absolutely alone. She felt forgotten, and so she ran.

Perhaps she was heading for Egypt, hoping to find relatives or someone who might care.

It wasn't an easy trip for a pregnant woman, so when she saw a spring of water in the desert, she sat down. She needed a drink, and probably a good cry.

Hagar Is Seen

What Hagar didn't know was that God hadn't forgotten her. And God was watching. God was about to seek out Hagar. God has an amazing way of finding people who feel forgotten.

Suddenly an "angel of the Lord"* appeared to Hagar. He called Hagar by name. The angel initiated a conversation by asking questions. "Hagar, slave of Sarai, where have you come from, and where are you going?"[3]

Hagar didn't have an answer for the question of where she was going. She had no good plan; she was just running away from her life situation.

The angel continued. He knew Hagar's issues. He knew she was pregnant. He even knew what the baby's name would be. He told Hagar about herself and about and her child's future.

---

*Some Bible scholars believe this "angel" was actually the preincarnate Son of God. So perhaps this was Jesus making an Old Testament cameo.

He assured her, "The LORD has heard of your misery."[4] Perhaps Abram and Sarai had forgotten her, but God had not forgotten her. In fact, the angel of the Lord told Hagar to name her son Ishmael, which is a combination of two Hebrew words, *shama* and *el*. *El* refers to God, and *shama* means "to hear." Ishmael means "God hears." So every time Hagar would ever speak her son's name, she would be reminded that God had heard her cry.

Think about how insanely revolutionary this conversation must have been for Hagar. She was not one of God's people. She probably didn't know God or even much about God. We have no reason to think she believed in God at all. But God sought her out. And in that moment, she knew that God, the one true God of Abram, was real, and that he was really for her. She was not forgotten.

In that moment, she gave God a name. Personally, it has never occurred to me to give God a new name. It seems above my pay grade. But Hagar had just had an extraordinary moment with God, and she punctuated it by naming him.

"She gave this name to the LORD who spoke to her: 'You are the God who sees me,' for she said, 'I have now seen the One who sees me.'"[5]

In Hebrew, the name she gave God was "El Roi."* El Roi means "the God who sees."

There are a couple of times in the Bible[6] when the presence

---

*I am desperately fighting the urge to make a joke about Hagar naming God after the boy in the cartoon *The Jetsons*. And the fact that the only other place I've heard the name *Hagar* is in the comic strip *Hagar the Horrible*. Must.fight.urge. Jokes.wouldn't.be.funny. Can't.hold.out.much. longer.

of God is represented by a figure that is covered in eyes. God is the God who sees.

The Bible also tells us that "the eyes of the LORD are everywhere, keeping watch on the wicked and the good."[7]

And "the eyes of the LORD range throughout the earth."[8]

We see this repeatedly in the life of Jesus. He noticed people no one else seemed to see. He saw the leper who was unclean, untouchable, and considered unworthy of attention. He saw the blind beggar that everyone else ignored. He saw the grieving widow. He saw the sick man chained as an outcast in a graveyard. He saw the invalid hoping for healing at the pool of Bethesda. He saw the children. He saw the insignificant old woman who had only two pennies to put in the offering.

Why? Because Jesus is God.

And God is El Roi, the God who sees.

Gary Is Seen

Gary was driving home in the middle of the night from his miserable job making people miserable to a home life he equally despised. He was listening to the radio when a commercial came on for a church.[*]

Gary rolled his eyes and changed the station. When the song ended, a commercial came on. It was the *same* commercial for the *same* church.

Gary was annoyed. He changed the station again. The song ended, and the *same* commercial came on for the *same* church.

---

*We started our church for people who had been forgotten by the church—for people other churches weren't interested in or weren't willing to reach out to. So we do radio ads, often in the middle of the night. Why? Because we know who is up in the middle of the night.

Now Gary was freaking out a little bit. He couldn't brush it off as a coincidence. He felt like someone was trying to get a message through to him.

Personally, I think he might be right. Maybe having the radio ad play three times on three different stations within three minutes and Gary's turning to those three stations in the perfect sequence at the perfect times was God's way of telling Gary, "I see you."

Gary decided to go check out this church. He told his wife, and knowing Gary's history of poor decision making, she insisted on going along to protect him.

On the day Gary showed up at church, my message was about how God is for those who have been turned off by the religious hypocrisy of those in the church. Gary had been turned off by the church and was stunned to hear that Jesus had the same aversion to religious hypocrites that he had. Gary decided to come back and learn more about this Jesus. He kept coming back, and he discovered that although he believed he was unworthy of being loved, he was loved perfectly by a perfect Father in heaven. Eventually Gary found himself with feelings of love he had never experienced—and those feelings were for God. Gary said yes to God, gave his life to Jesus, and was baptized.

You Are Seen

Maybe you've felt unseen and overlooked your entire life. You might feel unloved and even unlovable. Maybe those feelings have led you to a lonely place with tears as your only companions.

You are not alone.

God has heard your cry.

He is seeking you out.

Even if you are not of his people. Even if you don't know him or even much about him. Even if you don't believe in him at all.

He knows your misery.

He is real. And he is really for you.

He is El Roi.

The God who sees you.

You are not forgotten.

Who Else Is Forgotten?

Gary realized that he couldn't be the only one who felt forgotten. So now, imbued with God's love, he decided to seek out other forgotten people in the same way God had sought him out.

Gary started volunteering at a convalescent home. The home was filled with elderly people who had outlived their families or had been dumped off or disregarded by their families. He went from room to room, asking if any people wanted to share their stories.

Gary also started handing out cold bottles of water to homeless people on hot summer days. He chose the homeless, because people look at them but don't see them. Gary had always considered them lazy, smelly, drunk, drug-addicted bums who had chosen that life and wanted to stay in it. As he gave out water bottles and listened to people's stories, God changed his thinking and rocked his world. Gary's heart grew for this forgotten people group.

He wanted to do more. He started making lunches and giving them away. Someone at our church heard about what Gary was doing and asked if she could join him. Soon word got out, and a little team of compassionate people were making and handing out lunches to seventy or eighty homeless people every Tuesday.

One of the homeless people they gave lunch to was Angel.

Angel Is Seen

Angel was abandoned by his family early in life and grew up in and out of a string of foster homes. Later he found himself in and out of prison. After yet another incarceration, he decided he couldn't take it anymore. He had nothing and nobody, and so he ran . . . to Las Vegas.

The warm climate makes Las Vegas an attractive destination for the homeless, but that's not why Angel chose to go to Sin City. No, he thought of all the drunk people walking up and down the Strip with pockets full of gambling money and decided it was the perfect place to pick pockets. And that's exactly what he did.

One of the people Gary and his crew from our church handed lunch to week after week was Angel.

One day, after eating his lunch, Angel said he would like to start helping them. Gary and his friends smiled at the nice gesture and said, "Oh, sure. That would be great someday. We'd love that."

The following Tuesday when the group showed up at our church to make the lunches, Angel was standing outside waiting for them. They were stunned. Knowing his situation, they asked, "How did you get here?" He said, "I jogged." It was thirteen miles! He jogged thirteen miles to help them make the lunches!

He helped make the lunches, then went and helped serve them to the homeless.

Afterward, the crew thanked him, and he told them how much he appreciated them. Angel said he'd like to come check out their church sometime. They smiled at the nice gesture and said, "Oh, sure. That would be great someday. We'd love that."

So that Sunday, which happened to be Super Bowl Sunday, they showed up at Verve, and Angel was standing outside waiting for them. They were again stunned, and again they asked, "How did you get here?" And again, Angel said, "I jogged." Like, "I think we've gone over this. Duh." And just to make sure you're getting this: he jogged thirteen miles to be at our church service!*

Angel listened to the message, which was about how followers of Jesus need to share the gospel with others. In it, I suggested a few ways we can present the good news about Jesus. Angel responded. That day he accepted God's offer of forgiveness of his sins and gave his life to

---

*Some people don't show up at church if they didn't get their full eight hours of sleep; he jogged thirteen miles! Some people won't make an appearance on Sunday morning if they're having a bad hair day; he jogged thirteen miles!

Jesus. Along with ten other people, Angel got baptized that day.

Angel later told me that his plan for Super Bowl Sunday had been to pick pockets all day. It was the perfect day to make lots of money. But because Gary chose to let homeless people know they weren't forgotten, Angel's plan was radically changed.

Ever since, Angel's *life* has been radically changing.

Angel writes me letters and hands them to me on Sundays, telling me about how his life is transforming, how he's gone from feeling empty and lonely to being full and surrounded by a family who loves him. The letters are incredible.

Angel shows up at our church two or three times a week to clean the building. He never asks for anything. He just wants to serve.

Angel continues to serve with the little team of people who go out every Tuesday to love on lonely homeless people. He's become an integral member of that team.

In fact, they recently went to a meeting held by the Nevada Homeless Alliance. The purpose of the meeting was to bring together the various people and organizations seeking to help the homeless in Las Vegas. Members of the alliance spoke to the different groups represented. They then offered the microphone to anyone who wanted to share how they were serving the homeless. Gary was pretty surprised when he saw Angel walk up to the podium.

Angel leaned in and told everyone he was homeless. He

thanked them for their efforts. He shared his thoughts on what was working and what was still needed. He thanked them again and walked back to his seat.

The group was stunned. Never before had a homeless person attended a meeting of the Homeless Alliance. Getting the perspective of an actual homeless person was groundbreaking. They gave Angel a standing ovation.

After the meeting, the coalition members told Angel that a seat on their board was about to open, and they asked him to consider taking it. The police department asked Angel to become its spokesperson to the homeless, telling people about events and resources the department was offering through the new Corridor of Hope program.

Angel's life is changing, and he's helping to change the lives of others. And it's all because Gary let him know that he wasn't forgotten.

I think I knew God was for the forgotten, but Gary has been teaching me that *I* need to be for the forgotten as well.

This raises the question: Who do you know who probably feels forgotten?

The old lady next door?

The kid who sits alone every day in the cafeteria?

The older, single guy at church who lingers in the lobby, hoping for another conversation before he heads back to his empty apartment?

How can you be for them in a way that communicates that they are seen not only by you but also by a loving God?

Never Forgotten

When I e-mailed Gary and asked him if he had ever felt like a forgotten person, he explained that all through his life he had always felt forgotten. But then the tone of his e-mail changed dramatically. He wrote that he now knew that there hadn't been a single day of his life when God had forgotten him. He wrote:

> I think he was there right beside me all along, just waiting for my eyes and ears to open. In fact, I am sure he was with me when, as a small child, I underwent two major open-heart surgeries before the age of seven. God was with me the several times I tried to take my own life. God was by my bedside when I lay in the hospital after the OD and heart attack. God was with me when I found out that I was diabetic, a condition that went unchecked for months; my sugars were so high the doctors were amazed I wasn't dead. God was with me on 9/11 when I was in the area where the towers got hit. God was with me when I forsook my marriage, and he helped us get through it. God was with me when I hated my job, everyone around me, and myself. I just never paid attention, until one night I heard the radio ad.
>
> As for me, well, I know I am no longer forgotten. My past can no longer hurt me. I have made new friends who cherish me. I still have a motto for life, it's just changed: L.G.L.P.A.T.T.W.U.D.

"Love God, Love People, and Turn the World Upside Down!"

I am Gary, and I am no longer forgotten.

Neither are you.
Actually, you never were.

14

GOD FOR THE BROKEN

I'M GOING TO TELL YOU A STORY. There is a point in this story when you will think, *Wow, Vince is impressively brilliant*. But for most of the story you will be thinking, *Wow, Vince is colossally stupid*. I would ask you to focus on the brilliant part, but that choice is up to you.

One summer evening last year, we decided to grill steaks for dinner. I decided to try to make a chimichurri sauce to go with the steaks. I had never made chimichurri sauce. I had never eaten chimichurri sauce. But I had seen chefs prepare it on several food shows.*

---

*Yes, I watch food shows. (The girls and I get together, learn how to cook, do one another's nails . . .)

So I got a recipe* and bought my ingredients. I was ready, and I was excited. I would get to try chimichurri sauce, expand my cooking chops, and prepare a great dinner for my family.

It turns out chimichurri sauce is pretty simple to make. You take oil, vinegar, garlic, and parsley and blend them together. So I put all of the ingredients in the blender and started blending. Problem: the parsley was not getting chopped up. I stopped the blender, started the blender, stopped the blender, started the blender. It still wasn't blending. I shook the blender but to no avail. The parsley was fluffed up too high and wasn't packing down enough to reach where the blades were. I started out excited, but now I was getting frustrated.

So obviously I needed to get the parsley down by the blades. And I thought,** *Well, I'll just push the parsley down while it's blending.* So I pushed the parsley down and restarted the blender. Still not working. I pushed down more . . . and my finger got blended. I've cut my finger with a knife before. It was painful. I've hit my finger with a hammer before. That was painful too. But when a blender chops your finger, it combines the best of *both* of those injuries. You have the slice of a knife with the speed and blunt force of a hammer. Painful doesn't quite describe it.***

So I screamed. Actually, I shrieked.

The pain was so intense I thought, *I'm going to faint.* That

---

*You know, from one of the girls.
**Are you ready? This is the "Vince is colossally stupid" part of the story.
***If you want to say, out loud, "Vince, you are colossally stupid," I understand.

actually sounded really appealing. I could be removed from the pain and let someone else figure out how to stop the bleeding.*

The problem was that my wife wasn't home. It was just my two kids and me. And in that moment of absolute pain, I thought, *My kids are not going to be able to deal with this. If I faint, I will crash to the ground. I'll probably hit my head on the counter or the floor. So it won't just be my finger; my head will be bleeding too.* So,** in pain, blood spurting from my finger, about to faint, I had the presence of mind to dive to the floor, so if I fainted I wouldn't hit my head on anything.***

So I dove to the floor. But I didn't faint. I started yelling—okay, shrieking—"Kids, Band-Aids! I need lots of Band-Aids! It's a gusher!"

What was really depressing is that I had started out so excited. I'd had such high hopes, but they ended up crushed as I crashed to the ground.

Close to the Brokenhearted

Doesn't that seem to be the way life goes? You start out so excited.

As a kid, with your whole life in front of you.

Or when you make the team.

Or when you go off to college.

Or start a new job.

---

*While I slept like a baby.
**Are you ready? This is the "Vince is impressively brilliant" part of the story.
***If you want to, you can say, out loud, "Vince, you are impressively brilliant." After calling me colossally stupid, I think you owe me at least that.

Or get married.

Or have children.

You start out so excited, but often things don't go the way you thought they would. And you end up, not on a high, but very low, crushed and crashed to the ground.

Like everyone, I came into the world full of expectation. But very quickly that was driven out of me. I think back to one night when I ran downstairs and tried to pull my father away from my mother. In his rage, he had broken her piano and was now going after her. It was more than just a bad night. I was learning something about the fallibility of love and the instability of relationships. I was being taught not to trust but to live in fear. And as my father stormed out and my mother and I lay on the floor crying, I realized it wasn't only her piano that was broken. I was.

If life has left you or certain parts of your life broken, it may be helpful to realize that Jesus came into a broken world filled with broken people. In fact, that's *why* Jesus came. If the world were perfect, he could have stayed in heaven. But it isn't, and so Jesus came.

There's a verse back in the Old Testament that sheds light on why Jesus came. Psalm 34:18 says, "The LORD is close to the brokenhearted and saves those who are crushed in spirit." God himself comes close to the brokenhearted through Jesus.

Not only does he come close, but Jesus actually participates in our brokenness.

Perhaps an area of brokenness for you is your finances. You've been out of a job for a while. Or you have a job, but you just don't make enough to get by. Or you're still trying to climb out of a debt you feel buried under. Do you realize that Jesus was born into a poor peasant family? The Bible says, "Though he was rich, yet for your sake he became poor."[1] If you have financial problems, God knows how you feel.

Or it could be that you're feeling lonely. You may be doing quite well financially, you may feel successful in your career, but there's a relational deficit in your life. Feeling lonely doesn't afflict only people who are alone. You can live in a house with your spouse and kids and still experience abject loneliness. If you're feeling lonely, Jesus knows how you feel. His friends deserted him when he needed them most. One of his best friends, Judas, betrayed him. Jesus even had a moment on the cross when he felt deserted by God and cried out, "My God, my God, why have you forsaken me?"[2] Jesus understands the pain of feeling alone.

Perhaps your area of brokenness has to do with your family. Maybe there's a fractured relationship or some intense disappointment. Jesus knows all about dysfunctional families. In fact, soon after Jesus began his ministry of teaching and healing, strangers flocked to see him, but "when his family heard about this, they went to take charge of him, for they said, 'He is out of his mind.'"[3] At least your family has never accused you of being crazy and tried to drag you away from your job.*

Maybe the issue in your life right now is that someone you

---

*Unless they have, in which case, yeah, you really have family issues.

love has recently passed away, or you've received a scary diagnosis from the doctor. Jesus understands. We're quite sure his earthly father, Joseph, died when he was relatively young, and Jesus himself died when he was only thirty-three years old.

When Jesus came to earth, God came physically close to the brokenhearted, and he shared in their brokenness.

Saves Those Who Are Crushed in Spirit

It's not just that God understands.

In fact, you may be wondering: So God forgives bad people, we've established that—but does God fix broken people? Does he even know the pain I'm in? And can he do anything about it?

Those are important questions, and the answers are found in Jesus.

Jesus went to a town called Nain, and his disciples and a large crowd went along with him. As he approached the town gate, a dead person was being carried out—the only son of his mother, and she was a widow. And a large crowd from the town was with her. When the Lord saw her, his heart went out to her and he said, "Don't cry."

Then he went up and touched the bier they were carrying him on, and the bearers stood still. He said, "Young man, I say to you, get up!" The dead man sat up and began to talk, and Jesus gave him back to his mother.

They were all filled with awe and praised God. "A great prophet has appeared among us," they said. "God has come to help his people." This news about Jesus spread throughout Judea and the surrounding country.[4]

So Jesus was about to enter a town called Nain* and encountered a funeral procession. We don't know much about the situation. How did the widow's husband die? How old was this son? Did the widow have any daughters? We do know, almost certainly, that the son had died within the last twenty-four hours. Back then people were buried shortly after death because of the hot climate and the lack of formaldehyde and embalming fluids. So this mother had just lost her only son. The shock had started to wear off, and the most raw, deep moments of pain were beginning to set in.

And then Jesus came walking by. First, I want you to notice what Jesus felt. The text says, "His heart went out to her." This is translated from the word *splagna* in the original language of the Bible. I love the word *splagna* because it sounds like the noise someone makes when throwing up, as in, "Yuck, I am so sick. I just splagnaed all over the place." And that's actually what it means. Splagna refers to a person's intestines. The idea conveyed in this word is that of having your guts twisted or ripped out. It's the deep, wrenching, painful feeling you experience when you see something that

*And, by the way, when a person entered that town, they were: in Nain in the membrane, in Nain in the brain! (Sorry for that. And if you don't get the Cypress Hill reference, you're probably better off.)

is wrong and it moves you deeply. That's what Jesus felt when he saw the dead boy and the widow who had just lost her only son.

What's interesting here is that this was a very common scene. If you or I were walking down the street and we saw people walking and wailing and carrying a casket, we'd wonder what was going on, because it's not normal for us. But it was incredibly normal back then, almost an everyday occurrence—the equivalent to us of a hearse followed by a procession of cars. So this was a very ordinary moment, but Jesus had a very extraordinary reaction. He didn't just feel sorry for the grieving mother. He felt this woman's pain. His guts were ripped out. He felt splagna.

The second thing I want you to notice is what Jesus did. Sometimes we have an emotional reaction to someone's pain but we don't do anything about it. It could be that we don't care or that we don't know what to do. Well, Jesus felt something, and then he did something. He cared enough, and he knew just how to help.

So what did he do? He walked up and touched the coffin.

They didn't have coffins like we do, with sides and lids. For them, a coffin was just a flat piece of wood they laid the body on. My guess is that Jesus didn't walk up and touch the wood underneath the body. He probably touched the body.

Some amazing things happened in this moment. Jesus was crossing some boundaries that people of that time never crossed. The religious leaders back then had identified over five hundred laws the people were required to follow. For these religious leaders, it was all about following the rules. They were focused on keeping the outward appearance of cleanliness, rather than being concerned about actually being pure on the inside. And one of the laws was that you could not touch a dead body. Dead bodies were considered unclean, and if you touched one, *you* became unclean.

Jesus' heart went out to this woman, so he walked up, and ignoring the religious policies, he touched her dead son. It's like he was making a statement: "These religious boundaries would keep me from showing the compassion I must show, and so these boundaries must be crossed."

Jesus touched the boy, and the crowd must have gasped because of how shocking that was. But then something even more incredible happened—the boy began to breathe! Jesus' touch brought the boy back to life.

And indirectly it did something just as dramatic for the mother. Back then, a widow's only real hope was her son. If you had no husband and no son, it was very likely you would become destitute or have to do questionable things, horrible things to support yourself. If this woman had daughters, she would need even more money. Who knew what would become of those daughters? But Jesus touched her son, and he was alive again. And Jesus walked the boy over to his mother and handed him to her in an affectionate way. Jesus not only gave her back her son, but he also gave her back her hope, something she had very little of just a few moments earlier.

I want you to notice how Jesus felt and what Jesus did.

Because if you're broken, you need to know that he has splagna for you. When he sees your pain, his stomach turns and his heart goes out to you. You might think, *No. I doubt he even notices. Everyone is broken in some way. My situation is ordinary. There are bigger things for God to be concerned about.* Maybe so, but the beautiful thing about this story was that no one else would have noticed the funeral procession. Everyone dies eventually. There were lots of funerals happening every day. There were widows everywhere. The situation was ordinary, but Jesus noticed. And he didn't just notice; he cared. His guts were ripped out. And that's exactly how he feels when he sees your pain.

So what can Jesus *do* about your brokenness? He can fix it. He can bring healing. Jesus can bring hope, because he isn't someone who just lived; he's someone who still *lives*. And healing broken people isn't just something that happened; it's something that *happens*. If that's hard for you to believe, I understand. The fact that God is for the broken is (almost) unbelievably good news. God is for *you*. He is for the broken, and he can bring healing.

In this story we see him bring the dead back to life! You could argue that there's no healing more dramatic than that.

I could argue that we're also dead. I obviously don't mean *physically* dead. But when you're broken, it can feel like there's no hope in your life. I know. I grew up feeling dead. My father's abuse and the shame I developed left me feeling lifeless. Relationally, I struggled to develop friendships with any vitality. And emotionally, I felt like I had nothing. I didn't experience highs or lows. I just felt dead. As an adult, I was diagnosed with attachment disorder. Attachment disorder develops when a young child doesn't have the opportunity to bond with the people he or she should bond with. Experts don't consider it a behavioral issue but rather a kind of brain injury or brain damage, where neurons don't attach correctly. In fact, people who have attachment disorder are found to have smaller right hemispheres of their brains. When you do a brain scan on a person with attachment disorder, you'll see dead spots in places where there should be brain activity.

That's how I felt. Where there should have been life, there was just a dead spot.

Maybe your marriage is a dead spot.

Or your financial situation is a dead spot.

Or your career is a dead spot.

Or your self-esteem is a dead spot.

Or your relationship with your parents is a dead spot.

But the good news for us is that God can raise the dead. It's not just for people in Bible times, and it's not just for physically dead people.

Check out this prayer from the book of Ephesians: "I pray that your hearts will be flooded with light so that you can understand the confident hope he has given to those he called—his holy people who are his rich and glorious inheritance."[5]

The prayer begins with a desire that we would understand the value God places on us. Yes, we've screwed up. Yes, we're messed up. Yes, we're broken. But in a sense it doesn't matter, because God still views us as treasures. We are "his rich and glorious inheritance." God is for us.

The prayer continues: "I also pray that you will understand the incredible greatness of God's power for us who believe him. This is the same mighty power that raised Christ from the dead and seated him in the place of honor at God's right hand in the heavenly realms."[6]

How much power does God use in our lives and make available to us? Incredibly great power. Mighty power. It's like the power God used to raise Jesus from physical death to new life on the first Easter Sunday. He now uses that same power to raise us from death to new life.

In the next chapter of Ephesians we read, "Because of his great love for us, God, who is rich in mercy, made us alive with Christ even when we were dead in transgressions—it is by grace you have been saved."[7]

It says that we were "dead in transgressions." *Transgression* means sin.

This certainly refers to *our* sins. Our sin leads to our spiritual death—our separation from God.

But it seems to me that we can also be dead, or have dead spots, because of the sins of others. It might be the transgressions of an abusive father, an unfaithful husband, a dishonest business partner, or a hateful grandmother.

But there's good news. God can make us alive. Why does God want to help and heal and save us? Because of his great love. Because he is rich in mercy. Because he treats us with grace, which means we get the opposite of what we deserve.

We've screwed up, we're messed up, we're broken, but we're forgiven—because of grace.

Ephesians 2:5 says we are saved by grace. That word *saved* is written in the perfect tense.* Do you remember from school that verbs can be past tense, present tense, future tense, or a perfect tense?

Past tense indicates something that has already happened.

Present tense indicates something that is happening right now.

Future tense indicates something that will happen eventually but hasn't yet.

The perfect tense in Greek (the language of the New Testament) refers to something that has happened in the past but has an ongoing impact in the present and into the future. Using the perfect tense draws attention to the continuing effects of something that has happened in the past.

And how cool is it that *saved* is written in the perfect tense!

The idea is that you were saved from death, you have been made alive with Christ, in the past, but the effect of that is continuing in your life. God will continually do his resurrecting work in your life until it's finally complete.[8]

That means you never have to feel defeated. You should never give up. You are not permanently broken.

As I mentioned when I shared about the shame that saturated my life until I met Jesus, the healing I've received from

---

*I'm about to get really geeky on you, but you'll have to forgive me—my mother was an English teacher.

God has been gradual. Day by day I see signs of life in all my dead spots. I've often been frustrated that I'm still struggling and that God hasn't changed me as much as I had hoped. But rather than dwelling on my frustration, I've chosen to live in trust and an expectancy that God's perfect power is still working in perfect tense. And over many years of day-by-day change, my life is now dramatically different.

That can be your story as well. The idea we get from the passage in Ephesians is that on the first Good Friday, Jesus absorbed our death on the cross. Then, on Easter Sunday, he conquered it. He defeated our death by his resurrection. And that same resurrection-from-the-dead power is available to you. God wants to love you from death to life. He can fix your brokenness by applying the greatest healing force in the universe, his unconditional love.

Will You Let Him?

But he'll do that only if you let him.

There's a problem.

It would seem that when we're broken, we would be acutely aware of our dependence on God, and we would seek him with a sense of desperation. But sometimes it's when we're hurting and needing God the most that we're most averse to turning to him.

It may be because we blame him for what we're going through.

Or we might think we're self-reliant and can get through this on our own.

A couple of years ago, our kids got to the ages when we could leave them on their own. So one day I was at work, and my wife went out to do some grocery shopping. Our son, Dawson, went into our daughter's room to let her know that she needed to do her chores. Marissa didn't like it that her big brother was acting like he was her dad. She said, "Get out of my room."

"No," he said, "You need to do your chores."

She picked up our house phone and said, "Get out, or I will call 9-1-1," and pushed the buttons. Apparently she didn't realize that pushing the numbers was enough. A phone call isn't made by pressing the numbers combined with intent to call; it's made by *just* pressing the numbers.

The police answered. Marissa heard, "9-1-1. What's your emergency?" Shocked, she hung up the phone. A few minutes later there was a knock at the front door. The kids looked out and saw a police officer. They both freaked out, ran upstairs, and locked themselves in their rooms! Marissa called her mom and explained the situation. My wife left the store and rushed home to tell the policeman there was no emergency and to thank him for coming by.

Marissa didn't really intend to call the police, because she didn't really want their help. In the same way, too often we don't want to call on God, because we don't really want him to show up. Whatever the reason, when we're broken and need God's healing love, we very well may be trying to avoid him.

God is available. His love can heal you. But God won't force his healing on you. You need to give him permission.

You need to put yourself in Jesus' path and allow him to touch you. Think about that day outside the gate to Nain. There were probably several funeral processions within a few miles of Jesus that day, but only one dead boy was given new life and only one mother received hope. Why? Because they were in the path of Jesus. They were in a place where Jesus could touch the boy.

I made a new friend this year named Jack. He's a Las Vegas cab driver. He's not a Christian. I met him when he was pretty new to Vegas, and he was excited about how moving here would make his life better. That's not what happened.

He and I got together one day at a Starbucks, and he explained that his lifelong best friend had committed suicide a year before. Jack had lost another friend not long before that. He said he was broken and didn't know what to do.

We talked for a long time. And we met repeatedly at that Starbucks.

I told Jack that God is for us. Because of his love, God sent Jesus for us.

I told him the parable of the Prodigal Son. I shared how the son rejects his father and goes off in rebellion but eventually wants to come home where, to his surprise, his father invites him back with open arms. I explained that Jesus came to let us know God is inviting us to come home to him. Our lives change when we come home to a relationship with him.

At one point Jack said, "Well, I know I need something, because I feel like all this stuff has hit me, and it's like my life has caved in on me."

I nodded and asked, "Do you want to hear something cool? You just basically used a story Jesus told. It was about two guys who each build a house. One builds on sand, and the other on a foundation of rock. Then storms hit. Storms always hit. The guy who built his house on rock is sitting in his home safe and sound, thinking, 'It's too bad there's a storm.' But the guy who built his house on sand has his house collapse on him and finds himself homeless. Why? Because he chose to build his house on the wrong foundation."

One day we were about to walk out when Jack asked, "One more question. I just don't know how to get over the loss I'm experiencing with my friend dying and just everything that's happened. How do you deal with that?"

"Jack," I said, "imagine a child, maybe five years old, who is swinging high on a swing set. Suddenly he goes flying off, crashes to the ground, and breaks his arm. He starts screaming and crying in pain. His mother is nearby, sitting on a bench, so she comes running over. She holds him and whispers in his ear, 'I'm so sorry that happened. I know how bad it must hurt. But it's going to be okay.' His arm still hurts, but the boy calms down. The mother rushes him to the hospital. A doctor checks out his arm, puts it in a cast, and explains that it's going to be uncomfortable for a while, but the healing has already begun, and it will get better.

"Now imagine another child," I continued, "also five years old, also swinging high on a swing set. Suddenly he goes flying off, crashes to the ground, and breaks his arm.

He starts screaming and crying in pain. But this is a home-less boy. He has no mother nearby. No one to hold him. No one to tell him it's going to be okay. No one to take him to the doctor. So his arm will just stay broken. Healing will not happen."

Then I said, "Jack, *you're that homeless boy.* You're in pain. You're crying out. But you have no one to hold you. No one to tell you it's going to be okay. No path to healing. But what you do have is a God who loves you, who came for you, and who is inviting you to come home and into a relationship with him. He wants to be close to you and help you with your pain and anything else you'll ever go through. But he'll do that only if you let him. And that's the choice you have to make, Jack. Will you let him?"

The same is true for you. The Lord is close to the broken-hearted and saves those who are crushed in spirit. But only if you let him. Will you let him?

You might think, *But Jack wasn't a Christian. I've already said yes to God's invitation to come home. I've already moved into a relationship with him.* And that's great, but again, I've found that even as a Christian, often the times when I'm least interested in turning to God are the times when I need him most.

God wants to apply the greatest healing force in the universe and make you alive in your dead spots, but will you let him? Will you let him love you?

Pastor Michael B. Brown tells a story that illustrates God's love:

A friend told me about a boy who was the apple of his parent's eyes. Tragically, in his mid-teens, the boy's life went awry. He dropped out of school and began associating with the worst kind of crowds. One night he staggered into his house at 3:00 A.M., completely drunk. His mother slipped out of bed and left her room. The father followed, assuming that his wife was in the kitchen, perhaps crying. Instead he found her at her son's bedside, softly stroking his matted hair as he lay passed out drunk on the covers. "What are you doing?," the father asked, and the mother simply answered, "He won't let me love him when he's awake."[9]

God loves you.

His unconditional love is the greatest healing force in the universe.

It may not happen immediately, but he can fix your brokenness.

He can make you alive in your dead spots.

But will you let him?

15

GOD FOR EVERYONE GOD PUTS IN YOUR LIFE

In 1995, Operation Rescue, an aggressive pro-life group, moved their national headquarters. Their new location was next to A Choice for Women, a clinic that provided abortions.

The two foes were now neighbors.

I know what you may be thinking. It's the same thing I would think. *Oh boy. Here comes a bunch of conflict, none of which will help anyone. Protests, name-calling, confrontations in the parking lot.*

What actually happened *did* take place in the parking lot, but it's not what you would expect. It was less clashing over disagreements, and more bonding over the Beach Boys.

Operation Rescue had a somewhat famous director at the time, Flip Benham, an ordained minister who has long been active in the pro-life movement.

A Choice for Women had a more famous employee, Norma McCorvey. Norma was better known as "Jane Roe" from the *Roe v. Wade* case. That Supreme Court ruling gave women in America the right to have abortions, which gave rise to organizations like Operation Rescue.

Flip Benham noticed that Norma took smoking breaks throughout the day in the parking lot between their two buildings. He began venturing outside to spend time with her. As you might expect, she initially resisted him. Eventually his kindness and neighborliness wore down her defenses. The two developed an unlikely friendship.

During one of their affectionate but always lively conversations, Norma told Flip, "What you need is to go to a good Beach Boys concert."

Benham responded, "Miss Norma, I haven't been to a Beach Boys concert since 1976."

That response startled McCorvey. The idea that this "reverend" went to rock concerts made him seem human. Suddenly, he wasn't just a surprisingly nice neighbor; he was relatable.

Norma found herself more open to him, and as their friendship grew, she accepted an invitation to Benham's church. Then came the moment that shocked the world. On August 8, 1995, Norma said yes to Jesus, and Flip baptized her in a backyard swimming pool.[1]

And Who Is My Neighbor?

Toward the beginning of our journey together, I wrote, "Jesus loved to tell stories. His stories made people angry. People hated him for his stories. You could argue that it was his stories that got him killed."

We began with some stories Jesus told in Luke 15, provoked by the Pharisees and teachers of the law muttering questions about why Jesus would welcome and eat with sinners. We'll end with a story from Luke 10. Again the story was instigated by a question, and again the questioner was an "expert in the law."[2] He asked Jesus what he must do to inherit eternal life. Jesus responded to his question as he typically did—with a question.* He asked the man what he had read in the law. The expert replied, "'Love the Lord your God with all your heart and with all your soul and with all your strength and with all your mind'; and, 'Love your neighbor as yourself.'"[3]

"'You have answered correctly,' Jesus replied. 'Do this and you will live.'"[4]

You would think it would end there. The guy could brag about how he had the right answer, but no, Mr. Smarty Pants had a follow-up question: "And who is my neighbor?"[5] We're told he asked the question because he wanted to justify himself.

Apparently he had the right answer in his head, but in his heart there were people he didn't want to love.

---

*In the Gospels we see that Jesus was asked around 183 questions. He answered 3 of them directly. Jesus himself asked more than 300 questions. What does that say for how his followers should interact with nonbelievers? Maybe those of us who are so quick to give answers and spend so little time listening need to pray about tweaking our approach.

Jesus responded to his question with . . . a story. Of course he did. Jesus loved stories.

This story has become quite famous. You've probably heard it or are at least familiar with the title character. Unfortunately, it has lost its meaning over time. Let's think about what it meant to the people who heard it originally from Jesus, and we'll see that it means a lot for us today.

The story Jesus told has a certain structure sometimes called "the rule of three."[6] It's a story with three main characters, in which the first character does something, and the second character does the same thing, setting an expectation. But the third character does something surprising instead of following the pattern.

Jesus began, "A man was going down from Jerusalem to Jericho, when he was attacked by robbers. They stripped him of his clothes, beat him and went away, leaving him half dead. A priest happened to be going down the same road, and when he saw the man, he passed by on the other side."[7]

At this time, the road from Jerusalem to Jericho was notoriously dangerous. Robbers jumped this traveler, beat him, took everything, and left him lying on the ground.

Soon a priest, who was man number one in this rule-of-three story, came down the road. This road still exists today, and it's quite narrow. There are spots where people have to walk single file. The priest must have noticed the guy. But he chose to ignore him.

Why didn't the priest help the guy?

One possibility is that he was a priest. To serve in the

Temple, you had to be in a state of ritual purity, what they called being "clean." Back then the first rule in the *written* law concerning what would make you impure was contact with a corpse. The first rule in the *oral* law concerning what would make you impure was contact with a Gentile.

The priest saw this half-dead body on the road. *Half dead* was actually a technical term. Back then rabbis identified stages of death,* and this was a phrase rabbis used to describe the last phase before someone died.

In the first chapter, I mentioned the movie *The Princess Bride.*** At one point in that movie, the hero, Westley, is thought to be dead, and so his comrades bring him to Miracle Max. Miracle Max looks at him and says, "It just so happens that your friend here is only *mostly* dead. There's a big difference between mostly dead and all dead. Mostly dead is slightly alive." This guy on the road is mostly dead, so the priest might have thought that touching the man would make him impure.

In addition, the priest didn't know whether the man was an Israelite (a Jew) or a Gentile. Usually this could be determined by a person's clothing. But Jesus, brilliantly, included in his story the fact that the robbers stripped the man of his clothes, so the priest couldn't discern if this guy was one of "us" or one of "them." *Is he someone I'm supposed to be for or against? Is he someone I have to love or not?* The priest didn't

---

*As a pastor, I am grateful that "clergy" no longer identify stages of death. Yuck.
**Using *The Princess Bride* in both the first and last chapters is what comedians would term a "call back," what authors might call "bookending," and what you might think is . . . too many *Princess Bride* references! If so, I apologize profusely.

know. All he knew was that this was a human being in deep need of some compassion. But even so, the priest walked on by.

Then a Levite, who is man number two in this rule-of-three story, came along. The Levites were the people who assisted the priests in the Temple. "So too, a Levite, when he came to the place and saw him, passed by on the other side."[8] The Levite saw the man and walked right on by.

Two characters in a row did the same thing. The expectation was set.

There were many three-character stories in Jesus' time, often with the same basic three characters. First would be a priest. Second would be a Levite. They would both do the wrong thing. People loved that, because the religious establishment was not very popular. They wanted the priest and the Levite to be dumb and dumber. Then the third character would appear. He'd be the one who got it right. And the third character would *always* be an ordinary Israelite. People loved that, because they were ordinary Jews, and so the hero was one of them.

You can picture the crowd leaning in as Jesus' story progressed. They knew who was coming next, and they couldn't wait. Everyone was ready for Jesus to say, "But an ordinary Jew . . ." Except, that's not what Jesus said. Instead he dropped a bomb.

Jesus said, "But a Samaritan, as he traveled, came where the man was; and when he saw him, he took pity on him."[9]

Then along came a . . . Samaritan.

The Samaritans were the *enemies* of the Jews. The Israelites listening to Jesus knew who to be against, and it was the Samaritans. In fact, shortly before Jesus told this story, the Samaritans had defiled the Temple by taking rotting human bones and throwing them into the Temple courts.[10] The Jews despised Samaritans. There was nothing worse than a Samaritan, being with a Samaritan, or tolerating Samaritans.

And yet Jesus made the hero of the story a Samaritan.

This story is often called the parable of the "Good Samaritan." We still use that phrase: "She was being a Good Samaritan." Back then, no Jew would *ever* have used that phrase. There was nothing good about Samaritans. They were the ones God's people were supposed to be against.

This Samaritan broke the pattern. The Samaritan saw the man, had compassion on him, and stopped to help. He put the man on his donkey and took him to a town, where he paid to have the man taken care of. Whereas the priest and Levite did nothing, the Samaritan did everything in his power to help this stranger in need.

Everyone listening to Jesus' story was sitting in a stunned, confused, angry silence. Then Jesus turned to the religious expert who had triggered Jesus telling this story with his question, "Who is my neighbor?" Jesus responded to this man's question by taking out a hand grenade and rolling it into his lap. And then Jesus asked, "Which of these three do you think was a neighbor to the man who fell into the hands of robbers?"[11]

The expert in the law replied, "The one who had mercy on him."[12] Notice, he wouldn't even use the word *Samaritan*. To him it was a repulsive, four-letter word. Good people didn't even speak of those bad people.

Then Jesus reached over and pulled the pin on the grenade: "Go and do likewise."[13]

This is not a cute story about a "Good Samaritan." It's not a nice little story that we apply to our lives by helping old ladies across the street. This is an explosive story that contributed to Jesus being crucified. The "moral" of this story is that you should love the person you hate the most. The people you think are the most despicable are the very people you are most called to serve.

If Jesus were telling the story today, he might say a pastor came by and did nothing. Then a missionary came by and did nothing. But an abortion doctor . . .

Or a philandering liberal Democratic politician . . .

Or a drag queen . . .

Or a quick-to-debate atheist . . .

Or a pot-smoking hippie from Colorado . . .

Or an Islamic jihadist . . .

Whom Do You Least Want to Love?

Who is the person you *least* want to love and serve in Jesus' name? Who is the person you most want to be *against*?

That's the person Jesus would put in the story for you.

Jesus would tell you to "go and do likewise." He would encourage you to go to where that person is, to really see that person, and to have compassion on that person. He would challenge you to find ways to serve that person in the name of Jesus in order to let that person see God's love in you.

The people you think are least deserving of God's love may well be the people who need God's love the most.

This may be difficult for you. These are people you've always been against.

Understand: it doesn't mean their sin is okay. But neither is yours.

It doesn't mean they don't have things they really need to change. But so do you.

It *does* mean God is for them. And he is for you.

It means that *everyone* needs to experience God's unconditional and life-changing love.

If you've never experienced it, say yes, and you'll be revolutionized by it.

If you *have*, share it with others, and you'll change their lives. You'll change the world.

God is for the rest of us. He is wastefully extravagant with his love. Now go and do likewise.

As Scripture says, "Anyone who believes in him will
    never be put to shame."
For there is no difference between Jew and Gentile—
The same Lord is Lord of all and richly blesses all who
    call on him, for,
"Everyone who calls on the name of the Lord will be
    saved."

How, then, can they call on the one they have not
believed in?
And how can they believe in the one of whom they have
not heard?
And how can they hear without someone preaching to
them?
And how can anyone preach unless they are sent?
As it is written: "How beautiful are the feet of those
who bring good news!"

ROMANS 10:11-15

MY ABC BOOK OF PEOPLE GOD LOVES

THIS IS MY ABC BOOK of people God loves. We'll start with . . .

A: God loves Adorable people. God loves those who are Affable and Affectionate. God loves Ambulance drivers, Artists, Accordion players, Astronauts, Airplane pilots, and Acrobats. God loves African Americans, the Amish, Anglicans, and Animal husbandry workers. God loves Animal-rights Activists, Astrologers, Adulterers, Addicts, Atheists, and Abortionists.

B: God loves Babies. God loves Bible readers. God loves Baptists and Barbershop quartets . . . Boys and Boy Band members . . . Blondes, Brunettes, and old ladies with Blue hair. He loves the Bedraggled, the Beat up, and the Burnt out . . . the Bullied and the Bullies . . . people who are Brave, Busy, Bossy, Bitter, Boastful, Bored, and Boorish. God loves all the Blue men in the Blue Man Group.

C: God loves Crystal meth junkies,

D: Drag queens,

E: and Elvis impersonators.

F: God loves the Faithful and the Faithless, the Fearful and the Fearless. He loves people from Fiji, Finland, and France; people who Fight for Freedom, their Friends, and their right to party; and God loves people who sound like Fat Albert . . . "Hey, hey, hey!"

G: God loves Greedy Guatemalan Gynecologists.

H: God loves Homosexuals, and people who are Homophobic, and all the Homo sapiens in between.

I: God loves IRS auditors.

J: God loves late-night talk-show hosts named Jimmy (Fallon or Kimmel), people who eat Jim sausages (Dean or Slim), people who love Jams (hip-hop or straw-berry), singers named Justin (Timberlake or Bieber), and people who aren't ready for this Jelly (Beyoncé's or grape).

K: God loves Khloe Kardashian, Kourtney Kardashian, Kim Kardashian, and Kanye Kardashian. (Please don't tell him I said that.)

L: God loves people in Laos and people who are feeling Lousy. God loves people who are Ludicrous, and God loves Ludacris. God loves Ladies, and God loves Lady Gaga.

M: God loves Ministers, Missionaries, and Meter maids; people who are Malicious, Meticulous, Mischievous, and Mysterious; people who collect Marbles and people who have lost their Marbles . . . and Miley Cyrus.

N: God loves Ninjas, Nudists, and Nose pickers,

O: Obstetricians, Orthodontists, Optometrists, Ophthalmologists, and Overweight Obituary writers,

P: Pimps, Pornographers, and Pedophiles,

Q: the Queen of England, the members of the band Queen, and Queen Latifah.

R: God loves the people of Rwanda and the Rebels who committed genocide against them.

S: God loves Strippers in Stilettos working on the Strip in Sin City;

T: it's not unusual that God loves Tom Jones.

U: God loves people from the United States, the United Kingdom, and the United Arab Emirates; Ukrainians and Uruguayans, the Unemployed and Unemployment inspectors; blind baseball Umpires and shady Used-car salesmen. God loves Ushers, and God loves Usher.

V: God loves Vegetarians in Virginia Beach, Vegans in Vietnam, and people who eat lots of Vanilla bean ice cream in Las Vegas.

W: The great I AM loves will.i.am. He loves Waitresses who work at Waffle Houses, Weirdos who have gotten lots of Wet Willies, and Weight Watchers who hide Whatchamacallits in their Windbreakers.

X: God loves X-ray technicians.

Y: God loves You.

Z: God loves Zoologists who are preparing for the Zombie apocalypse.

God . . . is for the rest of us. And we have the responsibility, the honor, of letting the world know that God is for them, and he's inviting them into a life-changing relationship with him. So let 'em know.

NOTES

CHAPTER 1: GOD FOR THE REST OF US

1. Walter W. Wessel and Ralph Earle, Mark 2:15 footnote, in *The NIV Study Bible, 10th Anniversary Edition* (Grand Rapids, MI: Zondervan, 1995).
2. Luke 15:1.
3. Luke 15:2.
4. Luke 15:2.
5. Luke 15:10. See also Luke 15:7.
6. Jeremiah 4:19.
7. I also told the story about Dawson at the water park in *I Became a Christian and All I Got Was This Lousy T-Shirt* (Grand Rapids, MI: Baker, 2008). Adapted and used by permission of Baker Books, a division of Baker Publishing Group.
8. Jeremiah 4:22.
9. Jeremiah 4:1.
10. Luke 15:18-19.
11. Luke 15:20.
12. Luke 15:29-30.
13. Luke 15:31-32.
14. For a more thorough study of the three characters in Jesus' parable and of how the older brother rejected the father's love through his legalism, read Tim Keller's book *Prodigal God*.
15. Philip Yancey, *What's So Amazing about Grace?* (Grand Rapids, MI: Zondervan, 1997), 11.
16. See Matthew 11:19 and Luke 7:34.
17. See Luke 19:5.

CHAPTER 2: GOD FOR THE PROSTITUTES

1. Matthew 21:31-32.
2. Luke 7:36.

3. Luke 7:37.
4. Luke 7:38.
5. Luke 7:39.
6. Luke 7:40-49.
7. Luke 7:50.
8. Matthew 11:28-29.
9. Luke 7:48.
10. Luke 7:50.
11. See Hosea 3:1.

CHAPTER 3: GOD FOR THE SHAME FILLED
1. Mark 5:25.
2. See Leviticus 15:25-33.
3. Brené Brown, *I Thought It Was Just Me* (New York: Gotham Books, 2007), 5.
4. Ibid., 20.
5. Jean Baker Miller and Irene Pierce Stiver, *The Healing Connection: How Women Form Relationships in Therapy and in Life* (Boston: Beacon Press, 1997), 72.
6. Mark 5:26.
7. Mark 5:28.
8. Mark 5:29.
9. Brown, *I Thought It Was Just Me*, 242.
10. Mark 5:32.
11. Brown, *I Thought It Was Just Me*, 155.
12. Ibid., 32.
13. Mark 5:33.
14. Mark 5:34.
15. Brown, *I Thought It Was Just Me*, xxv.
16. Ibid., 32.
17. Ibid., 127.
18. See Psalm 46:1; 91:2.

CHAPTER 4: GOD FOR THE ADDICTS
1. Leigh Montville, *Ted Williams: The Biography of an American Hero* (New York: Broadway Books, 2004), 348.
2. See 2 Timothy 2:13.
3. Romans 8:31-34.
4. See Romans 5:6-11.

CHAPTER 5: GOD FOR THE DYSFUNCTIONAL FAMILIES

1. I also told this story in *I Became a Christian and All I Got Was This Lousy T-Shirt* (Grand Rapids, MI: Baker, 2008). Adapted and used by permission of Baker Books, a division of Baker Publishing Group.
2. See Mark 3:20-21.
3. Isaiah 53:3, NASB.
4. See Hebrews 2:14-18; 4:14-16.

CHAPTER 6: GOD FOR THE DOUBTERS

1. See Matthew 3:17.
2. Luke 7:28.
3. Mark 9:22 (italics mine).
4. Mark 9:23.
5. Mark 9:24.
6. John 20:25.
7. John 20:27-28.
8. John Ortberg, *Know Doubt: The Importance of Embracing Uncertainty in Your Faith* (Grand Rapids, MI: Zondervan, 2009), 137.
9. Luke 3:1-3.

CHAPTER 7: GOD FOR THE TATTOOED

1. I also told Tommy's story in *Renegade* (Grand Rapids, MI: Baker, 2013). Adapted and used by permission of Baker Books, a division of Baker Publishing Group.

CHAPTER 8: GOD FOR THE ATHEISTS

1. See Psalm 14:1.
2. See Romans 1:18-20.
3. Matthew 7:15.
4. Matthew 7:16-20.
5. Matthew 7:21-23.
6. John 13:34-35.
7. Philippians 2:15-16.
8. Titus 2:10.
9. James 2:14-17.
10. See, for example, James Martin, "Jesus Was Funnier Than We Think," *Relevant*, March 12, 2012, http://www.relevantmagazine.com/god/deeper-walk/features/28558-jesus-was-funnier-than-we-think.

11. Dionysius quoted in Rodney Stark, *The Rise of Christianity: A Sociologist Reconsiders History* (Princeton, NJ: Princeton University Press, 1996), 82.

12. Quoted in Joan D. Hedrick, *Harriet Beecher Stowe: A Life* (New York: Oxford University Press, 1994), 237.

13. For a detailed discussion of the many positive ways that Christians and the church have impacted society, including some of the ones listed here, see chapter five, "An Undistinguished Visiting Scholar," in John Ortberg, *Who Is This Man?* (Grand Rapids, MI: Zondervan, 2012), 59–73.

14. Nicholas D. Kristof, "Evangelicals Without Blowhards," *New York Times*, July 30, 2011, http://www.nytimes.com/2011/07/31/opinion/sunday /kristof-evangelicals-without-blowhards.html.

15. Philip Yancey, *Vanishing Grace: Whatever Happened to the Good News?* (Grand Rapids MI: Zondervan, 2014), 164.

16. 2 Peter 3:9.

17. 2 Chronicles 15:2.

18. Jeremiah 29:13-14.

19. Roy Abraham Varghese, preface to *There Is a God: How the World's Most Notorious Atheist Changed His Mind* by Antony Flew (San Francisco: HarperOne, 2008), ix.

20. Tim Keller, *The Reason for God* (New York: Riverhead Books, 2009) 130.

21. Quoted in Francis Collins, *The Language of God: A Scientist Presents Evidence for Belief* (New York: Free Press, 2006), 75.

22. Quoted in Antony Flew, *There Is a God*, 131.

23. Ibid., 78.

24. Ibid., 136.

25. Steve Paulson, "The Believer," *Salon*, August 7, 2006, http://www.salon .com/books/int/2006/08/07/collins/index2.html.

CHAPTER 9: GOD FOR THE WORRIERS

1. I also told this story in *I Became a Christian and All I Got Was This Lousy T-Shirt* (Grand Rapids, MI: Baker, 2008). Adapted and used by permission of Baker Books, a division of Baker Publishing Group.

2. American Heart Association, "Heart Disease and Stroke Statistics—At-a-Glance," http://www.heart.org/idc/groups/ahamah-public/@wcm/@sop /@smd/documents/downloadable/ucm_470704.pdf.

3. Matthew 13:7.

4. Matthew 13:22.
5. Craig Groeschel develops the idea of Christian atheists in his book *The Christian Atheist: Believing in God but Living as If He Doesn't Exist* (Grand Rapids, MI: Zondervan, 2010).
6. Matthew 6:24-34 (italics mine).
7. Matthew 6:33, NIrv.
8. Matthew 6:34.

CHAPTER 10: GOD FOR SIN CITY

1. Sally Denton and Roger Morris, *The Money and the Power: The Makings of Las Vegas and Its Hold on America 1947–2000* (New York: Vintage Books, 2002), 101.
2. Jonah 1:1-2.
3. Jonah 1:3.
4. See Jonah 1:5-12.
5. Jonah 1:17.
6. See Jonah 2:1-9.
7. Jonah 3:1-2 (italics mine).
8. Jonah 3:4.
9. Jonah 3:5.
10. Jonah 3:10.
11. See Matthew 28:19-20; Mark 16:15; Acts 1:8; 2 Corinthians 5:11-20; Colossians 4:3-6; 1 Peter 3:15.
12. See Matthew 22:37.
13. I also told Shawn's story in *Renegade* (Grand Rapids, MI: Baker, 2013). Adapted and used by permission of Baker Books, a division of Baker Publishing Group.
14. The best treatment of this topic I've read is in John Burke's *No Perfect People Allowed* (Grand Rapids: Zondervan, 2007).
15. Philip Yancey, *Vanishing Grace: Whatever Happened to the Good News?* (Grand Rapids, MI: Zondervan, 2014), 30.
16. John 7:37-38.
17. John 6:35.
18. John 4:13-14.

CHAPTER 11: GOD FOR THE PIMP

1. I also told Travis's story in *Renegade* (Grand Rapids, MI: Baker, 2013). Adapted and used by permission of Baker Books, a division of Baker Publishing Group.

2. John 8:4-5.
3. John 8:7.
4. See John 8:9.
5. John 8:10.
6. John 8:11.
7. John 8:11.
8. Romans 5:6-8.

CHAPTER 12: GOD FOR THOSE WHO HAVE BEEN TURNED OFF BY CHURCH
1. Matthew 23:1-5.
2. Matthew 23:13-15.
3. Matthew 23:23-28.
4. John 3:1-3.
5. John 3:16-17.
6. See John 19:38-42.

CHAPTER 13: GOD FOR THE FORGOTTEN
1. Genesis 16:2.
2. Ibid.
3. Genesis 16:8.
4. Genesis 16:11.
5. Genesis 16:13.
6. See Ezekiel 1 and Revelation 4.
7. Proverbs 15:3.
8. 2 Chronicles 16:9.

CHAPTER 14: GOD FOR THE BROKEN
1. 2 Corinthians 8:9.
2. Matthew 27:46.
3. Mark 3:21.
4. Luke 7:11-17.
5. Ephesians 1:18, NLT.
6. Ephesians 1:19-20, NLT.
7. Ephesians 2:4-5.
8. See Philippians 1:6.
9. Michael J. Brown, "First God Loves Us," in *God's Man: A Daily Devotional Guide to Christlike Character*, 2nd ed., ed. Don M. Aycock (Grand Rapids, MI: Kregel, 2000), 15.

CHAPTER 15: GOD FOR EVERYONE GOD PUTS IN YOUR LIFE

1. See: http://www.priestsforlife.org/brochures/whowasthejaneroe.htm, and http://en.wikipedia.org/wiki/Flip_Benham, and http://www.operationsaveamerica.org/misc/misc/aboutUs.html, and http://www.youtube.com/watch?v=tOcRxz3PT6Q.
2. Luke 10:25.
3. Luke 10:27.
4. Luke 10:28.
5. Luke 10:29.
6. I first learned about this story structure and the way it was typically used by Jews in Jesus' time from a sermon by John Ortberg.
7. Luke 10:30-31.
8. Luke 10:32.
9. Luke 10:33.
10. Information from that sermon by John Ortberg.
11. Luke 10:36.
12. Luke 10:37.
13. Luke 10:37.

ACKNOWLEDGMENTS

I would like to thank:

God. The fact that he has a particular soft spot for sinners is the only reason he was able to make a spot for me, and it's given me my life's purpose. I am humbled and grateful.

Jen. God gave me the perfect wife, best friend, and partner in ministry when he gave me you.

Dawson and Marissa. I thank God every day for giving me two amazing kids. It's unreal to think that God loves you more than I do! I can't wait to see the lives you're going to live for him.

The team at Tyndale, especially Ron Beers and Jon Farrar—for believing in me and this message that God is for the rest of us and for helping me to share it with the world.

Tony Young and the team at City on a Hill—for wanting everyone to know what God is doing at Verve and for how you're being the light of the world.

Don Gates. Thank you for partnering with me. You make it fun to walk through the whole process!

The Verve staff. I wouldn't have had the time to write a book, or have these amazing stories of life change to share in it, if it weren't for your hard work and dedication to bringing God's love to the rest of us.

The people who read this book in its earliest phases and helped to shape it: Aaron Saufley, Cherie Roe, Kevin Colon, Jennifer Antonucci, and especially Jane Vogel.

ABOUT THE AUTHOR

VINCE ANTONUCCI pastors Verve, an innovative church that seeks to reach people who work on and live around the Las Vegas Strip. The television series *God for the Rest of Us* chronicles Vince's work there. In addition to pastoring and writing books, Vince leads mission trips around the world, speaks nationwide, and performs stand-up comedy in Las Vegas. Most of all, he loves spending time with his wife, Jennifer, and their two kids.

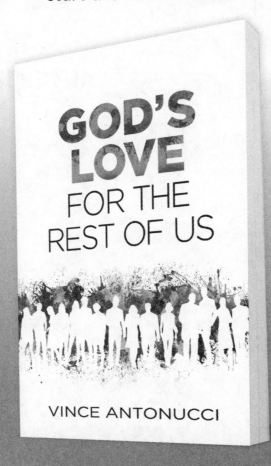

NEW RESOURCES FEATURING

VINCE ANTONUCCI
Verve Church, Las Vegas

Experience this powerful new study with your church, small group, or family and be inspired to see people – and yourself – as Jesus does.

20% OFF
AT CITYONAHILLSTUDIO.COM

USE CODE **GRBOOK20**

The Pharisees called Jesus,

"a friend of sinners."

He took it as a compliment. What would they call us today? Join the conversation.

TheRestOfUsResources.com